U

*"Like a Hole
in the Head"*

NEEDA

REVIEW

Nick Lyons Books

Some of the portions of this book appeared previously, as follows: "The Poem as an Action of Field," *Sewanee Review,* 1979; "Intertextuality," *Sewanee Review,* 1983; "Prefatory Statements, Prolegomenon, and Acknowledgements to Atomization of Criticism," *Sewanee Review;* "B/S: An Essay by Rodeo Barkis," *Sewanee Review;* "Excerpts from *The Awkward Book of American Literary Antidotes.*" *Sewanee Review,* 1982; "Olympian Ode for Jim Craig," *N.C. Wesleyan Series,* 1980; "Variations on a Theme," *Scholia Satyrica;* "A Leaf from *Wretched Richard's Almanac,*" *The Lamp and the Spine,* 1972; "Our Contributors," *Kayak,* 1978.

PRINTED IN THE UNITED STATES OF AMERICA

10 9 8 7 6 5 4 3 2 1

Library of Congress Cataloging in Publication Data
Schimmelpfennig, J. Parkhurst.
  Uneeda Review.

1. Literature—Periodicals—Anecdotes, facetiae, satire, etc.
I. Title   II. Title: Like a hole in the head.
PN6231.L55S35   1984   810'.8   84-21282

Cover and interior illustrations by Hank Blaustein

ISBN: 0-941130-03-7

UNEEDA REVIEW

"Like a Hole in the Head"

A LITERARY QUARTERLY DEVOTED TO POETRY, FICTION,

CRITICISM, AND ASKESIS

EDITOR
J. Parkhurst Schimmelpfennig, D. Ed.

MANAGING EDITOR
Bertha V. Nation Schimmelpfennig

POETRY EDITOR
Joyce Carol O'Schimmelpfennig

BOOK REVIEW EDITOR
Alyot Ferment-Schmidz

BUSINESS MANAGER
Ormond Hammerhead

SUBSCRIPTION MANAGER
Lady Vaseline Morale-Schimmelpfennig

EDITORIAL ASSISTANT
Hulga Fudge

ADVISORY EDITORS
Amelita Galli-Curci, Norman Vincent Pile, Hon. Warren J. Hamburger, Sigmund
Freud, Billy Martin, Malvin Belly, Eugene Onēgin, Leopold Bloom, Monte Carlo,
Grover Cleveland Alexander, Walter Jackson Bait, Ophelia Rehr, Lee Iacocca, Leo
Durocher, Leo Delibes, Sir Samuel Hoary, William Styrofoam, A. R. Almonds,
Geoffrey Heartburn, Mack Steele, Clifton P. Finnegan, Quasimodo, Tom Mix,
Bowie Coon, Rosalie the Coalquay Bore, Germ's Choice, Giovanni Martinelli,
David Coprophile, Call Me Ishmael, Rocky Gibraltar, Sandy Beech, Morris Friday,
Navarone Sunday, R. U. Horney, I. M. Inrutt, Oliver Silversmith, J. Uncas
Chingachgood, Marjorie Morningstar, Albert Canoe, Hans Castoff, Thomas
Sutpen, Smoot Hawley, Little Bilham, Stanley Cod, Al B. Senior.
   Editorial and Business Offices—Box 2345, Secaucus Polytechnic and Fine Arts
Institute, Veeneck, NJ 07001.

For matters of usage and form, authors should consult *Moby-Dick* and *Jane's Fighting Ships*. No footnotes, please; costs too much to set.

Unsolicited manuscripts should be accompanied by return postage and a check for $15 to cover handling costs, made out as follows: "Pay to Order of J. Parkhurst Schimmelpfennig and/or Bertha V. Nation Schimmelpfennig." No responsibility can be assumed for loss or damage unless packed in dry ice.

Uneeda Review is indexed in *PMLA; Burpee's Seed Catalog;* the *Index Expurgatorium; Psychopathia Sexualis;* M. Maimonides, ed., *A Guide to the Perplexed;* and *Who's Who in Baseball.*

Subscriptions: Institutional, 1 yr., $19.75, 2 yrs., $29.50, 3 yrs., anything over $35. Individuals, 1 yr., $.83, 2 yrs., $.97, 3 yrs., $1.15. Cash or foodstamps accepted.

Some items herein cribbed from *Kayak* and *Sewanee Review*, to whom much thanx.

Copies of all back numbers except the spring 1974 issue ("Poems of the Boudoir," v. 13, no. 2) are available at one subway token each from the Subscription Manager, c/o Section LL, Row J, Seat 7, Garden State Parkway, Veeneck, N.J. For an additional fee of $.25 the editor will autograph the lead editorial.

Authors are advised to copyright their own damned mss.

Contents

3

Editorial

Our 23 ½ Anniversary Issue

Time has a way, don't it? Difficult though 'tis to credit, the *Uneeda Review* is twenty-three years and six months old already yet. 1984—1974—1964—1960; *eheu fugaces, postume, postume, labuntur anni!* Or, *Ipsos custodies, quis custodiet?* Who, that is, takes care of the caretaker's daughter while the caretaker's busy taking care? Where are *les neiges d'antan?* Who is *d'antan,* and what does he want? If youth but knew, if age but could . . .

So, goddammit, we have come out on the other side. After all these years of boring from within. Years of the slow burn. Think of it! *We are the Establishment.* If only Charlie Glockenspiel were here to see it! April, 1960, down in the old Snack Bar (now the ladies' powder room); we were eating lunch; I with my customary salami and munster, Charlie as always with his Jello and beef jerky. "The state of letters," quoth he, "is flatulent. Something's gotta be done."

"True," said I. "What is more, we come up for tenure in the fall."

"You ain't just a-whistlin' the Goldberg Variations," he agreed. "It's bitter, bitter."

Muttering, I munched my munster.

"Whazzat you say?" Charlie asked.

"Sorry. Mustard. I need a dollop of mustard."

"You need a dollop of mustard"—he gazed at me, as from upon peakèd Darien—*"like a hole in the head!"*

I was puzzled, and must have looked it.

"Dontcha see? Thassit!"

"What do you mean, thassit?"

"I mean thass*it*, thass' what. The name!"

I was skeptical. "Name for what?"

"Think back," said Charlie, "to the day last September when I shown you my new epic poem in twelve parts, 'Schenectady Sidewalks,' and you shown me your article, 'Blithedale or Coverdale? Hawthorne's Covert Quest.' Too bad, you said, we don't have no place to publish 'em. And I said, mayhap we'll hafta start up a review. 'Member?"

Light began dawning. "And I said, 'What shall we call it?' And you said, 'We'll just have to come up with a good name.' Right?"

"Right! And we never did thinka one. But now we got it. You grab me?"

"Not exactly." I was slow in those days. "If we got it, what is it?"

"*Uneeda Review.*"

"*Uneeda Review?*" I still puzzled at his meaning.

"*Yoouuuuu—needa re-viewwwwww
like a hoooole—in tha heaaaad!*"

Oh, how we danced! Danced over to the chairman's office, to the dean's office, to the provost's office, to the president's sanctum. Told our dream. Money was plentiful then; those were the halcyon years. "Go to it, boys!" the chairman told us. "Could be," said the dean. "How much?" the provost asked. "Remember, not one word about politics goes into it," the president admonished.

The rest is history. That fall, on a foggy, foggy morning, Vol. I, No. 1 rolled off the press. Plaudits poured in. Allen Tate: "Thank you." Ernest Hemingway: "You want a fat lip?" Irving J. Krepstein: "Magnificent! A fresh voice at last! Please consider the enclosed sonnet sequence." Ezra Pound: "In cage/birdie no sing." Allen Ginsberg: "Some shit." J.

6

Hillis Miller: "Best of luck." James Dickey: "Do you pay?"

Unfortunately, Charlie Glockenspiel by then was not around to enjoy the fruits of our joint labor. In August he ran off with the chairman's wife, found a job teaching the Palmer Method to some Eskimos in Anchorage, Alaska, became a Caribou-hunting guide, joined the National Rifle Association, and died a heroic death at sea when the vigilante boat in which he was engaged in harassing a Save the Whales demonstration was stove in by a Coast Guard cutter and sank with all hands.

Upon my shoulders, therefore, has rested the responsibility for this review during all these years. They have, all in all, been good years. If the computer does not lie, during that time we have published 77 essays, 313 editorials, 220 poems, and 82 reviews discussing 274 books. No fewer than nine poems have subsequently appeared in book-length collections published under such distinguished imprints as Exposition Press, Pocohontas Books, and Hallmark Greeting Cards. Moreover, excerpts from two essays have been reprinted in *The New Yorker* as bottom-of-the-page items.

How much longer we shall be able to continue the good work I cannot say. As is all too well known, these are difficult days in the Groves of Academe. Our subsidy, never more than barely ample, has been cut in half. Library subscriptions are falling off. Our part-time secretary, Evalyn Shapiro Dimmock, has quit to have a baby. Thanks to President Reagan, the grant we used to receive from the East Rutherford Arts and Crafts Council is no longer forthcoming. Paper grows more expensive each year, and besides, the department's mimeograph machine has sprung a leak. Oops! There it goes again—

Yet that which we are, we are, an equal damper of erotic hearts, and if possible we shall keep the presses rolling and the literature gushing forth. Meanwhile, send checks. Make them out to Cash.

—J.P.S.

Otis Sistrunk

The Poem as an Action of Field: A Structuralist Experiment

I cannot claim that this piece was designed *ab ovo* for publication. Indeed, my first crude notes were reduced to writing merely as a means of trying to solidify the position of myself and other members of the "Carbondale Circle" (Vuk Brontosaurusky, Hoot Gibson Magruder, Fleur de Lysol-Javal, Hermaphrodite Briggs, Walter Ng, B. O. Súilleabháin, Mordred Teflon Squar, Dame Ursula Savage-Slaughter, K.G.B., Ropeyarn Sunday, Laser Taco, Roger Out, and the late Reverend Affirmative-Action Live-by-the-Scriptures). A luridly mutilated mimeographed "version" was pirated, however— probably by the same underachieving boors who tried so fecklessly to make me the laughingstock of the memorable Linda Darnell Festival at Bowling Green—and given wide circulation at the 1979 Ozone Park Conference on the Phenomenology of Phenomenal Phenomena.[1] What with the ridicule, the misprints, the transposed running heads, and all, I was made to look like—not to put too fine a point on it—an idiot. So here.

Regard, as preliminary to the problematic, the poetic opening of Eugene Field's post-symbolist "Wynken, Blynken, and Nod," subtitled "Dutch Lullaby":

> Wynken, Blynken, and Nod one night
> Sailed off in a wooden shoe—
> Sailed on a river of crystal light,
> Into a sea of dew.

Already (cf. "The Gross Lexicon in and per Se," ch. CLXXIII, pp. 853–922 supra) we have witnessed the horripilating potency of keynotes to establish at the outset of a poem the approximate range of its problematic and by im- no less than by ex- and com-plication, the concomitant range of its invariant solutions and isomorphically accompanying dissolutions. Hopefully the opening of the poem under examination—"Wynken, Blynken" etc.—asserts in such a "keynote" fashion the overall problematic of deterioration, beginning with the slippage of individual words from a condition of certainty (which we can denominate as the It) into a condition of obsolescence-suggesting decay (or the 't) and concluding with the slippage of (all?) persons from a state of wakefulness into a state of sleep. (A subsequent chapter will boldly probe the tendency of children's literature to will the induction of sleep and also the ambition of this causal feature of art to extend its boundaries far beyond mere entertainment for mere children. Art *as a whole,* it will be argued, takes for its final cause the hypnagogic production in each person of such a condition of fatigue, boredom, and peace that slumber is, regardless of the time of day or availability of cots, bunks, hammocks, sleeping bags, beds, floors, etc., irresistible. After all, the only surviving English cognate of "Shantih" is "coma." This enterprise clearly constitutes a subspecies of what the canonical motif-index[2] so aptly calls J2338, to wit, *"Mother sells child a bill of goods."*)

The manifold of complex deformations in Field's poem is balanced by a symmetrically binary manifold of complex redundancies. (1) The poem as a whole iterates the iambic rhythm (duhDUH), which is attacked perpendicularly by the repeated trochees (DUHduhDUHduh) of "Wynken" and "Blynken," but the threat of rhythmic deconstruction is disarmed or at least nonproliferated by the powerful presence, in the *same* verbal register or arena, of the *con*-struction of the perfect rhyme between the two words. (Much the same effect distinguishes the opening of Frost's "The Death of the Hired Man," which as a whole is in iambic pentameter; but the first line—"Mary sat musing on the lamp-flame at the table"—is neither iambic nor pentametric, so that the reader can be reinforcedly alarmed at the *de*-struction implicit in the basic syntagmatic sememe: "Mary sat . . . on the lamp-flame," which perforce enrolls her permanently, I should think, among those who favor fire.) (2) The poem proceeds by a general subsumptive strategy of placing each object as part of a more comprehensive context, but "Wynken" jeopardizes the success of that strategy by (a) shrinking the field of vision (as well as the vision of Field) to *one* eye of the natural, primal pair, and then by (b) coding that eye in terms of one of its functions, metonymically, a function, furthermore, that must necessarily remain the operation of *one eye and one eye only.* Two eyes, that is to say, cannot wink; that is the office of blinking, which, correspondingly, can be done by *two eyes only.*

Speaking of offices, by the way, I have carried out certain experiments with winking and blinking in the gossamer wings and corridors of randomly selected academic office buildings, and the only concrete result, apart from dismay, has been the congestion of my minute mailbox with a plethora of anonymous notes and mysterious clippings from unidentified peri-

11

odicals. One communication began enigmatically enough; "Can't you get it through your yellow-brick head that people like you are giving folk brain surgery a bad name?" but was attached to something that I must, in all humility, assume to be an honor: a handsome card certifying my membership in a body called "The Society of the Grand Prix." A number of the notes readily fall into that all-too-familiar category, J1803.2: *Prodigiously . . . prepossessingly . . . magnificently . . . incredibly . . . inconceivably pneumatic coed, with a one-digit SAT total, completely misunderstands the purpose of (I give you my word of honor) a strictly academic assignment.* For the convenience of orthodox folklorists, I have taken the liberty of classifying these communications (including telephoned limericks) according to motif:

G303.22.1. *Lost article with double inversion.* Smart old lady loses same BankAmericard fourteen times in same weekend; stupid young man finds same set of dentures fourteen times in same massage parlor.

H492.2. *Wife, mistaking husband for package of frozen kale, incinerates him and serves him to himself for dinner.* (See other entries under "Frozen Kale Tabu" and "Equal Rights Amendment")

H1334.4.1. *More Finns chew tobacco than Swedes.* A few Finns, however, persist in chewing Swedes.

J2311.7. *Cold hands and feet for the dead man.* His wife has told him that one tells a dead person by his cold hands and feet. He freezes his feet and hands and lies down for dead. Wolves eat his ass. "Lucky for you that his master is dead!"—Wesselski Hodscha Nasreddin I 225 No. 66.

K493.1. *Sportswriter fails to keep job by ambiguous syntax.*

K815.9. *Unusual spite.* Snake asks rabbit why he calls his car "a 1963 Oxymoron." Rabbit answers, "Because it's an old Nova." Snake eats rabbit.

K1443.6.1. *Debutante fails to recognize old family retainer.* Old family retainer clears things up with jocular allusion to unique birthmark, knowledge of which enables him to reveal self as absentminded archaeologist. Debutante gives back statuette, saying, "Retain *that,* you filthy old retainer!"

K1443.6.2. *Department stenographer in the dark about Lévi-Strauss.* Asks: "Hey, ain't he the guy discovered dungarees?" Long-suffering professor answers: "I believe he did."

P12.3.1. *Fiscal education.* Opossum gets "one up" on jackdaw by reporting him to the Internal Revenue Service.

V.351.1. *Media ecology.* The fate of the *Enterprise* hinges on the outcome of a personal duel between Kirk (William Shatner) and the lizardlike commander of an alien spaceship (60 min.).

X814. *Drunk men try to see one another home.* Absurd results.

But let us leave the slippery slopes of this iceberg and get back to the tip at hand. A simple graph of proximately successive paradigmatic modules will prismatically demonstrate both the range and the effect of the deformation or sequence of systematically patterned deformations inherent in "Wynken":

Wink	(1) Simple root *(radix simplex)*
Winking	(2) Suffix yielding complex verbal: gerund or participle? *(Ambivalenz)*
Winkin'	(3) Colloquial valorization via displacement of one phoneme by anudder

13

Winkin (4) Classic anapostrophe *(clinamen)*

Winken (5) Dutchification *(Nederlandischieren)*

Wynken (6) Semiperfected idiomorphic archaization (here Field stops)

*Wynkyn (*7) Perfected polyidiomorphic archaization (attested in certain printers' names etc., but scrupulously avoided by Field[3])

The parallel deformation *Blink-Blinking-Blinkin'-Blinkin-Blinken-Blynken* redoubles the horror of loss but halves the threat of *unique* monstrosity. By a process of mathematical induction, then, we arrive at a conclusive point: If deformation D can happen to one eye and parallelly to two eyes, then generalized deformation-function fD-summa can happen, my Lord, to any number of eyes at all; by a normative pun, what befalls I and then *we* can befall all. This maximalizing function is bound up tidily in the third term of the opening phrase—"Wynken, Blynken, and Nod"—which gives the endangered consciousness: (1) a restoration of the governing iamb, just now in jeopardy from a repeated and rhymed trochee; (2) a transumptive (i.e., of course, metaleptic) form of metonymy (the function of nodding standing for the whole existence of the head) without literal deformation (as in "ship's head"); and (3) the synthesizing presence of the setting or housing of both *eyes*—the wink *and* the blink—in one total capital function whose anatomy all but reverses the deterioration that has, constructively, eventuated in the dyad *Wynken* and *Blynken*, that is to say (as any child can see), a boustrophedon shuttling back and forth across a register composed of six terms, only one of which is "real": *Notton, *Notten, *Noddin, *Noddin', *Nodding, and, finally, *Nod* (verb and noun indifferently).

We must ask at the beginning, as with any instance of deformation, whether the changes be random or systematic, and, as before, metaphoric analogies cut much less ice as aids to analysis than metonymic associations. In an earlier volume (*From Half-Baked to Half-Digested: Styles of Radical Dyspepsia*, originally published as *The Irony of Myth: Three Stooges in Four Acts*), we have traced the genetic and etymological background of *hoax*, which, as we saw, depended on a ritualized (but desacralized) deformation in the shape of the following T-formation:

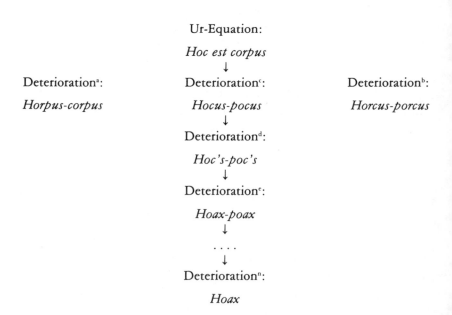

Ur-Equation:

Hoc est corpus
↓

Deterioration[a]:   Deterioration[c]:   Deterioration[b]:

Horpus-corpus   *Hocus-pocus*   *Horcus-porcus*
↓

Deterioration[d]:

Hoc's-poc's
↓

Deterioration[e]:

Hoax-poax
↓

. . . .
↓

Deterioration[n]:

Hoax

Obviously the very same serial deformation generates the tragic Cornish counting rhyme "Hickory, Dickory, Dock," which proceeds in a systematic-triadic manner (Tinker to Evers to Chance) by now utterly familiar to any analyst of ritual and myth:

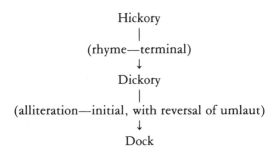

Hickory
|
(rhyme—terminal)
↓
Dickory
|
(alliteration—initial, with reversal of umlaut)
↓
Dock

or:

H i c k o r y	Cf. triads of "two-alike plus one-different"
D i c k o r y	(e.g., June-July-August) in G. Dumézil, *L'idéo-*
D o c k	*logie tripartite des Indo-Européens;* a fool and his money are some party.

—where the unconsumed residue, an *h* plus an *o* yields the *same* ultimate product as that generated by a conceivable "Deterioration²" on the base 0-grade *hoax,* namely, *ho.*[4]

II

. . . und ins verspätete Innre
unserer endlichen Frucht gehn wir verraten hinein.

Here, at least, we have come far from what Rilke pungently called "the retarded core of our ultimate fruit." For here the redounding counter-rhythmic couple "Wynken" and "Blynken" urge the poem in the direction of progressive deformation (and eye-formation) as well as deterioration, a motion subsumable ultimately as downward, i.e., in the direction of death, that which the souls in Poe-land mean when they moan "Nevermore." "Wynken" is the office of *one,* "Blynken" of *two . . .* and by induction and extrapolation the series con-

16

tinues all the way to "*Zynken"; but, in the shapely poem at hand, the urging set up by "Wynken" and "Blynken" is nicely balanced by an equal but opposite urging from the ominous "and Nod": (1) the iamb is asserted; (2) the binary matrix of two syllables contains now *two* words instead of one, and the two do not rhyme, although (if you have just spent a weekend locked in a room with no company but the cassette *Kenneth Burke's Greatest Hits*) their elemental literal components approach almost asymptotically the adumbration of an anagrammic pattern:

$$a \quad n \quad d$$
$$N \quad o \quad d$$

in which the *a/o* (alpha/omega) binary set is proffered alongside a set of *n*'s chiastically poised on the threshold of the terminal *d* that, significantly, concludes both words and calls up Bloom's vast accumulation of glosses on the *o/a* pattern in Freud's celebrated *"fort/da"* paradigm.

III

I realize that the text is of only marginal importance to such an analysis as mine, but I recognize as well that some senior citizens like a little vinegar with their greens—or, to put it another way, do not object to having their allegory spelled out somewhat. So here:

> Wynken and Blynken are two little eyes,
>   And Nod is a little head,
> And the wooden shoe that sailed the skies
>   Is a wee one's trundle bed.

In the final working out of the opposed urgings contigent on these "fishermen three" (i.e., three fishermen), two elemental settings of Special Space are sacramentally reached:

```
Wynken, Blynken-------------(dn)-------------Sea   −
Nod----------------------------(up)-------------Sky   +
```

(It will not escape your notice that up upside down is dn.) In this map Sea (which men traditionally go "down" to, although the canonical version would seem to want to read, "Men that go down *in* the sea in ships") embraces all the ingredients of deterioration, devolution, and entropy implicit in "fish," while Sky embraces those of valorization and, *mutatis mutandis,* improvement implicit in "star." Or in other terms:

	wooden shoe	fish
Three verbal——nominal forms	to catch	
	crystal slipper	stars

The combinatorial projections of maximum organic corruption (fish continuous with mankind) and maximum inorganic sanitation (star discrete from mankind, not counting such headlines as "Catfish Becomes Superstar"), the former being analogous-metaphoric while the latter is digital-metonymic, display and enact (and, of course, sanction) two opposed verbal and iconic developments:

$$+ \rightarrow - \quad \text{star-fish} \quad \text{starfish (singular with no distinct plural)}$$
$$- \rightarrow + \quad \text{fish-star} \quad \text{Pisces (plural with no operational singular)}$$

so that singularity is aligned with corruption in exactly the same measure as, paradoxically, plurality finds itself aligned with purification (*purificatio*), both alignments implicit in the problematic-paradigm of Williams' prophetic apostrophe to Governor Reagan: "It's a strange courage you give me, ancient star" but only ironically explicit in Stevens's corrective to the Rutherfordian quixotic star-netting: "An old horse." [The displacement of the marine-celestial axis from star-fish to star-horse is of the same order, though not of the same logical category or precinct of praxis, as the displacement of the inherent plurality of "Blynken" to refer to *one* eye *only*. This hub-and-spoke pattern can be precisely imposed on the network radiating spiderwise from bed (a hopefully dry place) to shoe (a dry object) to boat (a hypothetically dry system capable of containing within its parameters both beds and shoes), with such exactness of "fit" that Wynken and bed are joined as are (1) Blynken and shoe and (2) Nod and boat.]

At this point—*in articulo sapientiae,* as it were—the analysis touches another register of binary traffic between wet and dry, human and inorganic, plural and singular, harmonic and ironic:

Undifferentiated group of rocks in water
   \
     (process of enumeration and simplification—*katharmoi*)
   ↘
     Three rocks
       \
        (process of metaphoric-anthropomorphic attribution)
        ↘
         Trois sauvages
       /
       (bilingual pun + double paradox)
      ↙
      Dry Salvages

But such diacritical inquiry opens gates that must be saved for later chapters.

NOTES

1. At that conference, incidentally, it was noted by several prominent structuralists that there was something *very* fishy about Edward Mendelson's so-called checklist "The Writings of Mstislav Bogdanovich" (*TLS*, 19 December 1975). For one thing, a number of Slavic or Balkan items are impossible to find (e.g., *Filosoficky casopis*). For another thing, Mendelson suggests that Bogdanovich's profoundly seminal "Les structures heideggeriennes comme seul sujet de l'écriture" was published in *Grammatolexis* 2 (1970). Well, it was not. (Not not profoundly seminal, not *published*.) (At least not in that journal, long associated with the distinguished name of the Amsterdamkraal.) (Who is this Mendelson, anyway?)

2. There once was a Thompson named Stith who reduced every item of myth, song, fable, and mummery to a seven-word summary: no extraneous details, just pith.

3. Cf. *Dunciad* I. 149–50:

> There Caxton slept, with Wynken at his side,
> One clasped in wood, and one in strong cowhide.

Note, too, the alignment of metaphoric slumber, metonymic wood, and the suggestion of "winking" de Worde (i.e., slumber of words in the bed, or wooden shoe, of printing).

4. In *The Eugene Field I Knew* (New York: Scribners, 1898), p. 14, Francis Wilson quotes a rhymed address on the envelope of a letter from Field to another versifier:

> There is herein a plaintive ditty
> For E. C. Stedman, New York city;
> In Broadway, 66, fourth story,
> You'll find the same in all his glory.
> So take this packet to that Stedman,
> Or , by St. Hocus! you're a dead man!

Hocus (H. Formosus Clementinus) is well known nowadays as the patron saint of Zip Codes between 00001 and 59999 (inclusive).

Desmond Goohooligan

The Twenties: A Subliterary Memoir

Edited by Leonidas O'Dell

Editor's note: *The central role of Desmond Goohooligan in the intensely creative ferment that in the 1920s gave America its most exciting and accomplished literature is well known. The reviews and chronicles he was writing in such leading periodicals as the* Bell Telephone Times, *the* Proceedings of the Perth Amboy, New Jersey, Historical Society, Cap'n Billy's Gee-Whiz, *and above all, in the Fulton Fish Market* Daily Announcement Bulletin, *later collected in such magisterial compilations as* The Beaches of Sodom, To the Delaware Lackawanna and Western Station, *and* The Womb and the Beau, *not only defined the life of the decade as it occurred but provided a crucial form and substance to the otherwise mostly unharnessed and undisciplined imaginations of the writers of that day. Indeed, one comes to realize that without Desmond Goohooligan there might not have been any 1920s at all. We might have leaped straight from the Volstead Act to the Great Depression without so much as a racoon coat, a hip-pocket flask, a smuggled-in copy of* Ulysses, *or a monkey trial. Sinclair Lewis might never have published* Babbitt *and* Elmer Gantry. *There would have been no* Waste Land *(on the other hand there might also have been no* John Brown's Body*).*

America would never have known miniature golf or mah-jongg. Babe Ruth would not have hit sixty home runs. And so on. The thought is terrible to contemplate. Let us be thankful that Desmond Goohooligan was—and thus that the twenties were. [L. O.]

Introduction: *Desmond Goohooligan was born in Vincennes, Indiana (some say Illinois), on July 4, 1895, of prosperous parents. The elder Goohooligan operated a livery stable, and was of a philosophical bent: his son later recalled him as having a habit of staring up into the skies from time to time and remarking, to no one in particular, "It won't be water but fire next time." It was his mother who made by far the deepest impression upon young Desmond, however. A dominating woman, she once entered his third-grade classroom to scold his teacher for having awarded him only a B + on a composition (years later Desmond admitted that his mother had actually written the composition for him), and when the teacher objected, she picked up an inkwell from a desk, fired it through the open window, and forthwith removed the young Desmond from school. It turned out that this was fortunate, for the inkwell struck the school bully squarely in the chest, and had young Desmond remained in that school he would quite possibly have had the tar flailed out of him during recess. Shortly after this the Goohooligans entered young Desmond in St. Stanislaus Military Academy, Shawnee, Indiana, a highly prestigious school of the day. There his mother once again embarrassed him by calling him by his pet nickname, Snookums, right in front of the entire corps of cadets, eighty-one youths strong, and the nickname stuck to him for the rest of his life.*

Upon graduation from St. Stanislaus the young Desmond was enrolled at Cairo State A&M College and Normal School. Desmond was, as might be expected, an excellent student, and it was at Cairo State that he came, as it were, into his own. Swiftly establishing his intellectual superiority, he was elected as a freshman into the exclusive Robert W. Service Literary Society; was pledged to Alpha Sigma Sigma, the campus's most elite social fraternity; was appointed an editor of the campus literary publication, the Pharaoh; *was awarded the coveted Salmon P. Chase Medal for hortatory declamation; and in his senior year joined with F. Marion Crawfish in writing the annual musical production of the Square Club, which they entitled "Twenty-Three Skidoo; or, The Plucked Chicken Inspector."*

It was at Cairo State, of course, that he first met the future novelist Crawfish, and they became lifelong friends. Crawfish, with his contagious innocence, his infectious smile, and free spirit, looked up to Desmond for guidance and critical expertise. "Snookums Goohooligan was everything to me," Crawfish later said. "At that time I could not spell c-a-t; he had won the Indiana State Spelling Bee. I had done no reading of contemporary authors whatever; he could quote entire senten- ces from Ben-Hur: A Tale of the Christ, *and recite the poems of Edmund Clarence Stedman from memory. My favorite magazine was the* Sporting News; *he subscribed to* Delineator, *the* Police Gazette, Grit, *the* Congressional Record, *and other highbrow literary publications. Though he was something of a social neophyte, there seemed nothing in the intellectual world that he did not know about."*

In June 1918 the young Goohooligan was graduated from Cairo State summa cum laude, and was set to go to New York in pursuit of a literary career when a communication from Local Selective Service Board No. 3, Vincennes, forced an abrupt change in his plans, and he was inducted into the service of his country. Fortunately Desmond had learned to play the flute in high school, and he was straightway assigned to the 110th Regimental Band, Camp Lee, Virginia, where he rose to the rank of musician third class, and regularly played the obbligato in "Stars and Stripes Forever" until mustered out of service in February of 1919.

Proceeding to New York, where his friend F. Marion Crawfish was then working for an advertising agency, he too began looking for employment, and secured a position as assistant editor of the Fulton Fish Market Daily Announcement Bulletin. For that publication he soon began writing the regular feature entitled "Neptune's Nuggets," which quickly established his reputation in the literary life of Manhattan.

Something of the fervor of the literary life of the dawning 1920s may be seen in the comments he now began jotting down in the journal he began keeping, the first of 273 such volumes, each consisting of twenty-four ruled pages, bound in blue paper, with the words EXAMINATION BOOK: CAIRO STATE A&M COLLEGE AND NORMAL SCHOOL: Pledge printed upon the cover, that he was to fill during the years until his death.

F. Marion. Met F. Marion for lunch today at automat. He is writing a novel. Says his girlfriend at Cairo State, Ophemia Mulligan, won't marry him until he has $250 in the bank. Poor guy, thus to prostitute his art. Marion has zest, Marion has talent, Marion has, one might even say, genius. But Marion lacks discipline. And Marion loves Ophemia.

Kaskaskia. Began work on final portion of epic poem last night. There are those who say the epic is dead for our time. Little do they know. I have written three-fourths of one already, and the concluding section will be the best of all. Homer wrote his *Iliad,* Virgil his *Aeneid,* Milton his *Paradise Lost,* Longfellow his *Evangeline,* and I am writing *Kaskaskia: A Tale of George Rogers Clark.*

Hoboken Ferry. Crossing Hoboken Ferry today: towers of Manhattan like gigantic molars, canines, and bicuspids in the yawning mouth of the universe. *S.S. Berengaria* passed us en route, huge, four stacks, bound for the fabled places of the world. Stentorian blast of her whistle: a guttural bullfrog growling its "brekekekex co-ax co-ax" to the tugboats and lesser craft. Gulls dipping, diving, dancing astern, a-one, a-two, a-three: Welcome O life.

Wild Party. Strange party at the Clancy T. Ogburns' last night. F. Marion, Ophemia Mulligan, others. Ophemia a bit giddy: insisted upon drinking champagne from F. Marion's shoe. (F. Marion wears size 11½ C.) Got terribly drunk. Climbed upon piano and began singing "Rocked in the Cradle of the Deep" in falsetto. F. Marion somewhat embarrassed. Asked him how it felt to step into shoe recently filled with champagne. "Like diving into a bowl of warm oyster stew," he said. Must remember that. Afterward we all rode subway to Jones Beach, walked under stars. En route Ophemia Mulligan and F. Marion disappeared in direction of deserted bathhouses. Caught up with us half-hour later. Must have had something to talk over. Poor Marion. He doesn't even *like* champagne.

Conan Doyle on Gosse. Overheard fascinating literary anecdote while lunching at Nedick's today. A. Conan Doyle and Joseph Conrad were walking along pathway in Hyde Park when Edmund Gosse came by. After he passed out of earshot, Conrad turned to Conan Doyle and asked his opinion of Gosse. "You mean that cad?" Conan Doyle replied, and pointed down to the ground where Gosse had just been walking. "Mr. Conrad, those are the footprints of a gigantic hound!"

Marion Crawfish. F. Marion and Ophemia are engaged to be married. James Rodney & Sons has accepted Marion's novel, offered $250 advance, will publish in spring. Marion in fine spirits. One can only hope . . .

Burlesque. Went to Minsky's last night. The women bumping and grinding, the men looking on. The vacant gaze in the eyes of old men at burlesque: of what are they thinking? Of their lost youth? Helen of Troy? Jewish comedian comes out, tells smutty stories. In his weary features the long sad history of Semitism. The girls. Each attired in spangled scanties, with silk fringe along edges. Large bosoms all. Voices from the balcony: "Take it off! Take it off!" They will never take it off, not all of it, and that is the fascination. A nervous titter runs through the audience. "A shudder in the loins engenders there/The broken wall, the burning roof and tower/and Andrew Mellon dead." (That is not quite right; must look it up.)

Nature and Art. If Art is Mimesis, *i.e.,* imitation, then what is life? We learn through imitating others. So if we live through imitation, is life art, or is art life? *Cf.* Wilde: Nature imitates art. Holding the mirror up to nature, etc., and vice versa. The artist in our commercial industrial civilization is thus forced to imitate models of business, financial success. Why not, say, poem on crossing into New York City on ferryboat? Certainly as poetic as climbing Matterhorn, seeing Eton College. Hmmm. Why not?

Crossing Hoboken Ferry

Crossing the harbor where gulls dip and dive
let us fret not nor worry—
but be glad to be alive
for the sour past is o'er—
The flood tide crests the shore
and the Chrysler Building towers
where once were leafy bowers.
What of Egypt's crumbled walls?
Does the dust lay thick in Tara's halls?
Crossing over from Hoboken
What care I if Troy be broken?

Pretty good for a start. Could make a fine poem of this, I think.

Walt Whitman. Told Marion and Ophemia Crawfish of my poem. Ophemia, in her usual know-it-all fashion, insisted poem already written on approximately same subject by W. Whitman. Oh, well. One can't always be original. Will try something else.

Virginity. Ophemia C. asked point-blank last night if I was a virgin. Told her none of her business. Poor Marion. [This entry is, to say the least, enigmatic. Was Desmond still a virgin? The evidence, to the extent that there is any, indicates that it is possible. But one never knows. *L. O.*]

Desmond Goohooligan's lifelong enthusiasm for languages is manifested in the incident that follows. Before his death, he was to know no less than seventeen languages and a score of dialects as well.

Gullah. Puzzling encounter with Negro at fish market today. Was helping out behind counter when a large broad-shouldered black approached. "E hab eny pawgie?" he asked. (I reproduce the sound as best possible.) I could not make out what he wanted. "Pawgie," he kept saying, "pawgie, paw-giefeash. You en gnaw pawgie? Disy size." He spread his hands to indicate a length of about seven or eight inches. "Pawgie en too fat tru e belly, but e tall dough," he said. "E ab fawktail, yallow pless side e cheek. E berry good. Sweet like swimp." Try as I could, I was unable to make out what he wanted. Tried to sell him some tautog but he would not buy. "En go eat no pizen Yankeefeash," he said. "Buckra eat um mebbe." Or something of the sort.
    Later consulted Professor Trent at Columbia. He identified

speech as something called Gullah, which he said is commonly spoken on sea islands along coast of South Carolina. Considered to include African survivals, Devonshire English, West Indian vowels, diphthongs. Fascinating to think that within geographical boundaries of this nation a language unintelligible to most Americans survives. Also discovered that there are not one but two states in Union named Carolina—North and South. Very odd. Would be interesting to investigate strange political events that brought this about. Wonder if same species of English is spoken in both?

The arrival of the poetess Ellen Sestina O'Shea in New York sent many of the city's literary folk into a tizzy, among them Desmond Goohooligan, as the several entries that follow indicate.

Ellen O'Shea. Party at the F. Marion Crawfishes. Interesting girl there. Writes poetry. Offered to show her some of mine, said would be most interested. Very demure, but given moments of oddness, as when abruptly grasped candle from mantelpiece, borrowed my penknife, cut away tallow from butt end to expose wick, lit both ends of wick, and grasped center of candle between teeth much like dog carrying bone. Before evening was out, did same with every candle in the house. Strange. But charming, all in all.

Ellen O'Shea. Invited Ellen O'Shea to dinner at Child's— wanted to show her I appreciated gourmet food. She dressed in white gown with black spots, much like leopard pelt. Straw hat. Brought ms. of my epic poem, "Kaskaskia," to read to her. She suggested we go to my place afterward, and would read it there. When we arrived, she removed shoes, took seat on couch, asked me to read. Sat on chair opposite her, began, she stripping butt ends off candles and lighting wicks all the while. (I had laid in a supply of several dozen candles in event of this possibly happening.) Said I read divinely, but voice was too low; would I sit next to her on couch so could hear better. I did so, continued reading. She objected to overhead electric light, said hurt her eyes. She held double-lit candle between teeth, suggested I place head on her lap, read from there. Felt awkward, though found could read, but melting wax from candle kept dripping onto ms. Requested she tilt candle in other direction. Would I prefer she blow it out entirely? she asked. I said could not read very well in the dark. She said if candle tilted other way, wax would drip on her new dress. Did I mind if she removed dress? I said all right. She removed dress, replaced candle in teeth; I resumed reading. After awhile she said candle about to burn out at both ends. Told her not to worry, had plenty more. She said she was tired, would I object if reading continued in bedroom. She lay down on bed, lit up another candle. I drew up chair alongside. She said could hear better if I lay down next to her with head on pillow. Did so. She said light hurt eyes, would I mind if blew out for awhile. I said could not read in dark, suggested she place handerchief over eyes. She said tired of poetry for now. I said I also had draft of novel, could read that instead. She said never mind, was getting late, must be going. Replaced dress, shoes, I escorted her home in taxi. Thanked me for memorable literary evening. [A footnote to Desmond's relationship with Ellen Sestina O'Shea may be found in a cryptic comment made by Ophemia Crawfish in letter to Sara Murphy, dated 2 May 1924: "Ellen O'S. says spending evening with Snookums G. was like taking of tiffin-and-tea with Pope Pius XI." *L. O.*]

Slang. Overheard this use of American vernacular while riding Fifth Avenue bus:

"Hot today."
"You know it."
"It's not the heat, though, it's the humility."
"That's what they say."

Amusing Repartee. Heard this story. Nicholas Murray Butler and William Dean Howells were lunching at Century Club and Butler was telling about a Greek tailor who did his mending for him and with whom he always held converse in Greek. He had torn his pinstripe trousers getting out of a taxicab, he said, and he carried them to the tailor the next day. "Euripedes?" the tailor asked. "Yes," Bulter replied, "eumenides?"

F. Marion. The following song was composed by Marion Crawfish, with some assistance from me. A good deal of the effect depended on the appropriate gestures that accompanied every line, and on the impersonation of William Jennings Bryan, who was supposed to be singing it. Bryan, for some reason I do not understand, always seemed to Marion somewhat comic.

> It was back in old Nebraska
> 'Bout half way to Alaska
> That I started my glorious career
> I was left out in the cold
> Till I thought of the Cross of Gold
>   (you've heard about it)
> You could hear all those Democrats cheer.
>
> Oh I'm William Jennings Bryan
> My heart is like a lion
> And I'm running for Pres-i-dent
> And I'm very, very fri'ndly,
> But I sure hate Bill McKinley,
> So it's Bryan for Pres-i-dent!
>
> It was by the river Platte
> Where I knew that I was at
> That my words first excited all the town
> And they sure did have some fun

When I yelled, 'fifteen to one!'
(oh don't you know it)
Going to tear that Gold Standard down!

Chorus: Oh I'm etc.

Whether or not Desmond was indeed a virgin in his earlier career in New York, as Ophemia Crawfish has hinted, we can say with assurance that this no longer remained true after November 1927. For in his journal for that date and for several entries afterward, Desmond describes what is clearly a sexual liaison with a girl whom for simplicity's sake we shall call Inez, though that was not her name. She was, as we shall see, of working-class background—and it seems undeniable that it was this that made it possible for Desmond to enter into a physical relationship with her. All his other female acquaintances had been, like himself, from the upper reaches of society, and one guesses that the formidable influence of Desmond's mother was not without its role in his inability, at this stage in his life, to develop intimate relationships with any of them. Now for the first time Desmond encounters a girl of plebeian upbringing, and the result is a tender and happy interlude in his otherwise mostly unfortunate love life. Indeed one could wish that Desmond's background and social assumptions had not been such as to preclude a more lasting relationship with Inez. It is interesting, too, that within four years after Ulysses *was first published, and while D. H. Lawrence was still employing euphemisms, Goohooligan's boldness in describing his sexual experience foreshadows much of the explicitness of latter-day literature.*

Inez. Had for some time become accustomed to having dinner at Bijou Cafeteria, and had struck up acquaintance with waitress named Inez. Petite, olive-hued, sly smile, large round eyes, quaint manner of speaking, e.g., ''How about a lamb choppie, old chappie?" "Better have some of that lemon meringue. It's awfully good for your rang-a-tang-tang!" "Wanta second cuppa cawfee to drive away the collywobbles, dearie?" etc. Was raining tonight, and happened to be taking taxi just as she was leaving. Offered to give her lift. "You know," she said after being seated, "I like you." I replied that I was flattered that she did. Wished to know if I had what she referred to as a "steady girl." I said not at present. "No fooling? What do you do when you w**t y**r a***s h****d?" I explained that I lived in an apartment house with oil heat. "No, you dope," she said, "what I mean is, where do you go when you n**d s**e p***y?" I explained that one of the codicils in my apartment lease forbade the keeping of cats on the premises. "Well, for crying out loud," she said, "ain't you a card?" At this point she made the nature of her reference more nearly clear, and the result was that we retired to my apartment.

Inez. Have taken to "inviting" Inez to my apartment several times a week. Now that we have established a reasonable degree of frankness in our relationship, it is no longer necessary that she employ metaphoric or euphemistic terms to denote certain hitherto-unmentionable objects. She refers, for example, to her th**g (a word I forebear to translate, other than to suggest that it is the English equivalent of the Latin *res*). Asks whether my m*ck*y (using a common Irish diminutive) is st**nd**g (participial form of the Latin word *stare*). A physiological climax is always spoken of in the infinitive form of the English equivalent of the first verb in Caesar's famous summation, *veni, vidi, vici.* And so on. Must say that I had no idea that American vernacular could be used with such richness of reference and yet with such precision.

Ophemia C. Made the mistake of mentioning my liaison with Inez to F. Marion, who in turn was so indiscreet as to allude it to Ophemia. To my embarrassment she declared upon my arrival for dinner last night that she understood that I had decided to surrender my chastity at last. Informed her in no uncertain terms that it was "no affair of hers." "Thank the Lord for that," she said. Poor F. Marion.

Husband. Upon arrival at Bijou Restaurant last night found Inez in highly nervous state. "Don't look directly at me," she said in low voice. "He's outside watching through the window. Act like you're ordering dinner." Noticed that her eyes appeared to have been blackened and her lower lip somewhat swollen. Seems that her husband, who had been incarcerated in Sing Sing until recently, had come by the restaurant last night and had ascertained that she was not working late, as she had told him, and had been waiting for her when she returned home from my place shortly after eleven. Expressed my sympathy, had dinner of liver and potatoes, lingered over lemon meringue pie and coffee, read newspaper, then departed. Out of corner of my eye noted rather sturdily built chap standing near window observing me, but fortunately a taxicab was waiting at the curb. Hastily got in and closed door behind me. Oh, well. Shall have to take meals at another restaurant for awhile. *Sic transit gloria mundi.*

By 1929 Desmond's rising literary prominence was such that his every review and essay was eagerly read and widely discussed. The publication of Eliot's The Waste Land *several years before had revolutionized the poetry world, and it is not surprising, therefore, that when in October Desmond was sent abroad by the Fulton Fish Market* Daily Announcement Bulletin *to report on English marketing techniques in his now-famous "Neptune's Nuggets" column, he was eager to meet and to discuss matters of common interest with Eliot. His journal entries for the period are of especial interest in view of his subsequent writings on the subject.*

London. Odd how British drive their automobiles. Unlike pattern in United States, traffic proceeds along left rather than right side of street. Therefore, much confusion, honking of horns, etc.

Trafalgar Square. Went for walk today, arrived at Trafalgar Square. Noticed rather tall, soberly dressed man, umbrella under arm, standing atop pedestal of Nelson Monument, some thirty feet above pavement. Seemed to be staring into space. Upon drawing closer realized it was the poet Eliot himself. "Hello there, T.S.!" I called up. "What are you doing up there?" Seemed not to notice me, so I called again. "Mr. Eliot! Are you writing a poem up there?" This time he looked down, but said only, "Go away." I was about to explain my presence when a policeman came up (the British appear to refer to them as boobies) and suggested that I move along. Not wishing to cause a disturbance I did so. Curious business.

T.S. Eliot. Another fortuitous meeting with T.S. Eliot. Was in fishmonger's this morning inspecting merchandising techniques, when tall, soberly dressed man, umbrella under arm, came in. Recognized him at once. I reached into nearby tub, grasped large lobster, and held it out, saying, "I should have been a pair of ragged claws, eh, T.S.?" He frowned, turned, and departed the premises.

Traffic. The mystery is solved. Upon taking taxi to boat train this morning I realized that the controls and steering column are placed at the right side of the cab, not on the left as with ours. Surely that must be why traffic in Britain proceeds to the left rather than the right.

When Desmond Goohooligan returned to his native land aboard the S.S. Majestic *in late November of 1929, he found that much had changed. The stock-market crash had touched off the business panic that swiftly became the Great Depression. Though he had not himself invested in the market, his friends had been affected by the new turn of events. The riotous extravagance and waste of the twenties had come to an abrupt and catastrophic end. The F. Marion Crawfishes were in Europe, where Marion was valiantly battling his own addiction to malted milk and the growing signs of serious instability on the part of Ophemia. "Ophemia," Marion wrote to Desmond, "is writing a novel"; to Desmond the news only confirmed what he had long suspected. It was not long before the influential comments that he was making each week in his column "Neptune's Nuggets," which until then had had exclusively to do with literature and the arts, took on a distinctly political and economic cast, which as the business crisis deepened became more and more collectivist in tone. In late 1930 Desmond made the crucial step: he resigned from the staff of the Fulton Fish Market* Daily Announcement Bulletin *and became an associate editor of the* Lower West Side Literary and Socialist Beacon. *The 1920s were over; the 1930s were begun; unlike H. L. Mencken and other influential figures of the twenties Desmond Goohooligan had the sense to realize it. But that is another story, to be told in a future volume of Desmond's journals.* [L. O.]

Michelangelo Bermudas

Intertextuality

In place of a hermeneutics
we need an erotics of art.
—Susan Sontag

—I am a thing in a dustjacket trying
To make you read. Your eyes are soft and small
And want to scan an old text not at all.
They long to look at real men, standing, lying . . .
But twig yon volumes of back issues dying
In the remaindered pallor of the moon;
For I must feel the touch of such eyes soon,
I am a thing in a dustjacket trying.

—I am a ms. brand-new in beauty waiting
Until some young stud comes, and I do too.
But what grey tome along the stacks are you
Whose tones are dry as grass upon the lawn?
Out of my lap, you bore, before I yawn!
I am a ms. brand-new in beauty waiting.

Joyce Carol O'Schimmelpfennig

Eventual Eventail

the fan the
fan fans fans
the fan

as

back

ca su al
ca us al

us

un ti ed
un it ed

it

et
cet

uh
ruh

Northcote Fricassee

Prefatory Statements, Prolegomenon, and Acknowledgments to Atomization of Criticism*

This book forced itself upon me while I was trying to balance my checkbook and it probably still bears the marks of the desparation with which a great part of it was composed. The indulgent reader will overlook the occasional scribblings such as "Penny's bill 2 mos overdue" and "from now on J. W. Dant instead of Jack Daniel." After completing the grading of forty-five freshman term papers in two days I determined to apply the principles of 'l'esprit chasseur" which I had learned from the late Lionel Trilling to another aesthetic problem, involving the use of saliva on curve balls by Gaylord Perry or Don Sutton, preferably on a day when either was chewing paraffin instead of bubble gum, so that there would be no question of adhesive substances being imbedded in the seams. I therefore began a study of the modern history of the spitter, beginning with Bill Doak, Burleigh Grimes, and John Quinn Picus, only to discover that it was impossible truly to distinguish, from an archetypal point of view, my arse from my elbow.

*The editors of *Uneeda Review* are proud to present this excerpt from the distinguished literary critic Northcote Fricassee's newest book of criticism.

The basis of argument became more and more discursive, taking in such mythic deliveries as the slippery elm ball and use of a concealed nail file to abrade the horsehide covering. I soon found myself entangled in those parts of pitching that have to do with such words as "slider," "sinker," "change-up," and "Steinbrenner," and my efforts to make sense of these concepts in various published and unpublished exposés met with enough opposition to encourage me to take up crocheting. Yet I persisted. Eventually the theoretical and the practical aspects of the task I had begun completely separated, thanks to a timely warning by Gaylord Perry that if I mentioned his name one more time in connection with violation of 3.02, *Official Rules of Baseball,* concerning the illegal use of the spitball, he would punch me in the teeth.

> no player shall intentionally discolor or damage the ball by rubbing it with soil, rosin, paraffin, licorice, sandpaper, emery-paper or other foreign substance

and also 8.02,

> The pitcher shall not: (a) (1) Bring his pitching hand in contact with his mouth or lips while in the 18 foot circle surrounding the pitching rubber;
> . . . .
> (3) expectorate on the ball, either hand, or his glove;
> . . . .
> (6) deliver what is called the "shine" ball, "spit" ball, "mud" ball or "emery" ball. The pitcher, of course, is allowed to rub the ball between his bare hands.

What is here offered is pure critical theory, and the omission of all specific examples—even, in three of the four essays, of designation by such phrases as "a veteran right-handed pitcher born in Williamston, N.C., and recently employed by the Seattle Mariners"—is not only deliberate but absolutely craven. The present book seems to me, so far as I can judge it at present, to need a complementary report concerned with practical criticism, a sort of chrestomathy of pitching cozenage, assembled with the assistance of high-speed cameras, micro-enlargement, infrared sensory apparatus, litmus paper, depth flashers, and rubber gloves.

*　　*　　*　　*　　*　　*　　*

Let me, then, talk plain. Aristotle, in the *Poetics,* declares that "the greatest thing by far is to have a command of metaphor." Criticism has always been somewhat embarrassed by the statement: its patently moral assumption—that it is *good,* as opposed to being *evil,* to command metaphors—is not only Platonic in its derivation but Neo-Thomist in its cognition. What I suggest is that the emphasis should be placed upon the word "command"—at which suggestion all difficulties vanish, for not licence but restraint is the Stagyrite's* concern. It will be seen, therefore, that the concept of controlling one's metaphors is of venerable antiquity indeed. In precisely the same way—for all gall is divided into three poets—the spitball, being a metaphor, is not itself a *genre* (as the word is commonly used) but a *subgenre.* For historically it is an *offshoot* (not to be confused with the archaism *inshoot*) of the *curve,* which in turn is an offshoot of the *twist* of the hurler's arm. It will be seen that at any early stage of its development the *twist* was a Herculean (to mix one's mythos) effort to impart both velocity and veer to a pitched ball. Thus in its earliest forms a *twist* was perforce the product of a *twister—* which is to say, a *whirlwind.* Naturally it was associated with the concept of Deity, and it is thus evident that in the Greek figure of Aeolus, who kept his wind in a *bag,* we have the archetypal representation (or imitation if one prefers) of the reality of the *twister* (also augured in the Hebraic Voice from the *Whirlwind*). Therefore Aeneas and his Trojan wanderers,

---

*Who dat? (Ed.)

compelled to confront the *winds* of Aeolus, constitute an early but potent exemplar of the archetypal baseball team impelled to bat against the *twists* of a pitcher with a *bag* of tricky deliveries. It is not surprising, therefore, that the mythical proportions of such *Ur-twisters* (i.e., divinities) as Amos Rusie, who between the years 1890 and 1898 won 233 games for the New York Giants, were of a magnitude that was awesome in its heroic proportions. (The similarity to the Northern European figure of Thor, *hurler* of thunderbolts, is all too apparent.) Such figures have an important place in baseball literature, but as a rule are located outside the normal confines of time, place, and statistical verification. (For one thing, the pitching distance between mound and home plate was indeterminate.)

But as the historical imagination replaces the avowedly mythic and religious forms, the *twister* becomes the typical hero of romance, whose feats are marvelous but who is himself identified as a human being. At the same time a degree of specialization is introduced. Thus we identify the *curve* and the *spitter,* and identify too the hero exhibiting these prodigies of delivery as *curveballer* or *spitballer.* In the first category may be placed, *par excellence,* the figure of Christy Mathewson (1880–1925), known as "Big Six" (or, in Latin, "Magnum Sex") because of his possession of a *bag* of six distinct pitches. (The analogy to *sex* should be remarked, as in the connotation of *potency, performance, high hard one, base on balls,* etc. Those merely historical critics who have erroneously identified the appellation as an allusion to a well-known hook-and-ladder fire engine known as "Big Six" quite miss the archetypal significance of the term.) It is not surprising, therefore, that the particular pitch with which Mathewson is identified should be known as the "fadeaway"—that which disappears, in contravention of physical laws of motion, just as it reaches home plate. For Mathewson, who in popular legend did not drink, smoke, or stay out late at night, is the Hero, the

White Knight. (i.e., *Christ, son of Mathew;* in Arthurian terms the grail seeker, possessed of the magic sword but human nonetheless.)

Against the heroic but mortal legend of the *curveballer,* however, there evolves simultaneously the *doppelganger,* the antithetical yet satanically effective figure who by deceit and black magic effects the discomfiture of the White Knight-Hero, through crafty manipulation of the *spitter.* Where the powers of the *curveballer* are benign, harnessing the Aeolian bag of winds through techniques which, no longer supernatural, achieve quasi-marvelous results, those of the *spitballer* partake of the dark arts, and are archetypally excretory in derivation (spit-urine-faeces, as in the common baseball expression, "I can't hit that shit he's throwing out there"). Emblematic of the figure of the *spitballer* is Ed Walsh (1881–1959), who won thirty-nine games in the 1908 season for the Chicago White Sox (but later, *Black* Sox). It is demonstrative of the malevolent potency of the *spitballer,* drawing as he does on the blasphemous powers associated with the Evil One, that Walsh (i.e., Welsh—see Lady Charlotte Guest, *The Mabinogion,* in particular the figure of Math, the *wizard,* and also the expression "to welsh"; the sportswriting phrase "mound wizard" becomes obvious) won more games during a single season than the White Knight, Mathewson, ever did. Yet as always in the Manichean duel between Hero and Anti-hero the Forces of Light ultimately prevail, and the malevolent weapon of the *spitballer* loses its potency. Thus in 1913 Walsh developed a sore *arm* (cf. the Fisher King) and thereafter *faded* from the scene, while the good *curveballer* ends up with a lifetime total of 367 victories.*

*It is predictable that Mathewson becomes a military Hero in the First World War, is *gassed* (i.e., vanquished by *foul* ether), and later dies at Saranac Lake, New York, a tuberculosis sanatorium whose emblem is the red cross—but a *double* cross. Thus the Red Cross Knight, having figuratively *pitched* his sword into a lake, dies by the *waters.* See Lord Raglan, *The Hero;* Malory, Tennyson, etc.

42

Thus we are, by a notably commodious vicus of recirculation, brought back to the Modern Era of baseball. In the pages that follow I shall demonstrate the persistence of these archetypal patterns, hoping thereby to reforge the broken links between creation and knowledge, art and science, myth and concept, pitcher and catcher, and academic rank and tenure. May I caution that I am not proposing a change of direction or activity in criticism; I mean only that if critics adopt my concepts, Erich Auerbach, René Wellek, and Cleanth Brooks will be, to speak metaphorically, left out on their butts in the snow.

*　　*　　*　　*　　*　　*　　*

I am grateful for the generous encouragement given to scholarly research by the dean of the faculty of Caswell County, North Carolina, Community College, Dr. Lonnie Joe Stith, Ed. D., who by reducing my class load to four courses during the spring term of the 1978–1979 school session afforded me leisure and freedom to deal with my protean subject at the time when my checking account was at its lowest ebb and my Exxon card temporarily under suspension.

For financial assistance that enabled me to study at Three Rivers Stadium and to tour with the Seattle Mariners during the entire eastern portion of a road trip during the 1981 season I am indebted to the award of a Trailways vacation-special bus ticket and two books of food stamps by Mrs. Osmond B. Kratz, of Roanoke, Virginia, known familiarly to our family as Aunt Bessie.

My thanks go to the librarian of Caswell County Community College, Miss Irma Fulwider, for her tiresome help in sifting through the voluminous reference shelves of the library, and in particular for calling my attention to Bartlett's *Familiar Quotations,* Stevenson's *Home Book of Verse,* and the *Guinness Book of Records.*

About the translations. All the translations from Sanskrit and Bengali are my own responsibility. For the translations from Polack and Wop I am indebted, as are numerous scholars, to the Messrs. Joe Garagiola and Tony Kubek.

Many colleagues have generously contributed their time and effort to making this book a reality. In particular I should like to acknowledge the assistance of Dr. Fenley B. Goldblatt, chairman of the Department of Physical Sciences and Homemaking Skills of Caswell County Community College, for consultations on various theoretical problems associated with my research; and of Mr. A. C. "Stinky" Kleinschmidt, pitching coach of the Siler City Blue Sox, for his patience in elucidating the more practical aspects of my subject. Thanks, too, to the ever-obliging secretary of our humanities and social sciences division, Ms. Nina Pinopolis, for deciphering and transcribing my chickenscratch.

I am grateful, too, to my mother, Mary Ann Fricassee, now Mrs. Douglas P. McSwine, and to my stepfather, whom she married when I was seventeen years old, and also to the United States Navy, in which I enlisted three months later.

For permission to quote from published material I am indebted to the following: Basic Books, Inc., for *The Origins of Psycho-Analysis: Letters to Wilhelm Fleiss, Drafts and Notes, 1887–1892,* by Sigmund Freud, ed. Marie Bonaparte, Anna Freud, and Ernst Kris; Simon and Schuster, for *When Your Child Is Ill,* by Samuel Karelitz, M.D.; Samuel Green, for *The Day of Doom,* by Michael Wigglesworth; J. B. Lippincott, for *Ten Nights in a Bar-Room,* by T. S. Arthur; L. C. Page and Co., for *Pollyanna Grows Up,* by Eleanor H. Porter; the Universal Library, for *Studies in European Realism,* by George Lukacs; Grosset and Dunlap, for *The Sports Encyclopedia: Baseball,* by David S. Neft, Roland T. Johnson, and Richard M. Cohen; *Burke's Peerage;* the *Congressional Record;* Charles E. Tuttle Co., for *Read Japanese Today,* by Len Walsh; Charles Scribner's Sons, for *The Little Shepherd of Kingdom Come,* By John Fox, Jr.; Dover Publications, for *Guide to Southern Trees,* Ellwood S. Harrar and J. George

Harrar; the *Book of Mormon,* by Joseph Smith et al.; the *Caswell County Bugle,* Mr. R. D. Gunnels, editor and publisher; *Antiquities of the Jews,* by Flavius Josephus; and *The Sporting News.* In addition, I am grateful to Ms. Ruth Ann Snipes, chairman of the women's physical education curriculum of Caswell County Community College, for permitting me to consult her as-yet unpublished manuscript, *15 Easy Exercises to Keep You Strong and Healthy During Menopause.*

Finally, to my wife Crystal and six darling children my debt is beyond repayment. I may only recite their names, in order of chronological appearance, five sweet girls and a handsome little boy: Celia, Clarissa, Camilla, Caroline, Cordelia, and Oedipus, and declare, in the words of Samuel Johnson, ''a man will turn over half a library to make one buck.''

''Alazon Farm''
Siler City, North Carolina
January 1, 1983

J. Parkhurst Schimmelpfennig

Olympian Ode for Jim Craig

Man comes and tills the earth and lies beneath.
What goalie ever died with all his teeth?
O body swayed to panic, O worsening luck—
How can we know the pucker from the puck?

An Essay by Rodeo Barkis

B/S

Translated by Leonard Scott-Mongoose

Translator's note: This remarkable fragment of an essay was discovered among the effects of the late Rodeo Barkis. To judge from certain allusions in the text, it was composed during Barkis's late residence in America, and left uncompleted upon his subsequent return to his native France. *Quel dommage!* L.S.-M.

Audacity of text, that tells us, I signify this, I signify that! Audacity that borders upon the presumptuous, that would restrict our experience to what *he* desires. As if there were a decree that we must abjectly bow down to him. Text, who do you think you are? Who gave you this authority? Don't you know that even *Malbrouck s'en va t'en guerre* must be translated over again each day of our lives? Text, I announce to you, in all humility, that we are free! That we need no ukase, no passport embossed in gold and stamped in red in order to concern ourselves with you.

Who wrote you, text? Not that old scoundrel whose name you pronounce together with your title. He may have been a good man, text, but he relinquished all rights and privileges to you when he encoded you into those *a*'s, *e*'s, *i*'s, *o*'s, *u*'s you wear like so many road markers. Text, you are no longer his—and what is more, let me tell you what is so: *You never were!* For just as long as I choose to will you into existence, you are *mine* (I am yours), and therefore you would do well to heed me. And is that so cruel a fate for you? We two have so much in common, do we not? Shall we not therefore make a pact? If you will promise to remain yourself, I will in turn permit you to have existence only as me. Only do not presume to tell me what you *mean*. As well tell me what you do *not* mean; the one will serve as well as the other, since both of you, text and antitext, have everything in the world to say, but it is I who will say it, not you.

Tyranny of the text, that presumes to own us, when it is we who pour into his pathetic little black curves and lines the life that allows them to exist. Text = TYRANT. When, but for our intercession, text = TRY, ANT! A mere insect! Was it some Egyptian priest of the dead who first scratched those little marks into soft mud of the Nile, whereupon the cruel sun hardened them into impudent existence, and they became the Word? I AM, said the text. I AM WHAT I AM,* and thereafter none have dared controvert his tyrannical assertion. Man was born free, said Jean Jacques, but everywhere he is in chains. And why? Because he has allowed himself to be browbeaten by the text. The history of western man is the history of text-worship. Text has called himself Akhnaten, Jahveh, Christ, Caesar, Bonaparte, CIA; and his message has always been THEREFORE BOW DOWN!

It is time that we speak up. Four millennia of priestly death-worship are long enough. It is time to inform the text that his little game is over, that we have finally wised up. Henceforth we who make the text possible shall give the orders. And our first command shall be: There shall no longer be any commands—either by us or by the text. Henceforth it will be of no use for the text to come dressed up in vellum and tooled Morocco leather and in red-and-gold embossing and

*Here the reference is unclear. Did Barkis have in mind an allusion to Exodus 3:14, I AM THAT I AM, or to the well-known words of a comic strip character? L.S.-M.

pretend to a timeless ineffability in order to assert his dominion over ourselves. We are on to his clever charade: we shall be hornswoggled no more.

Be it therefore agreed that text is a plurality. There is not The Text; there is only text. The plurisignification of text ensures that there can be no logic, no grammatical structure, no inert order of words. What text says to me is multiplicity, a multiplicity that withholds even as it offers. I am the detective, who will ferret out the clues for myself. It is only I who may do so, for the privilege of overhearing is mine alone. Others may also overhear, but it is their text, not mine, that whispers to them. I possess the exclusive right to my text, which I gladly share with all even while I hoard him lovingly for myself alone. Coyly text presents himself in the bedroom of my desire, modest in his promiscuity; text bids me caress him, but in the long silence of lovemaking passively asserts his otherness. *Lie with me,* he says; captivate me with your falsehood. In our duplicity we consummate the passive autoeroticism of our mutual sexuality. Text = SEX: a penetration. In each other's embrace we reenact the outrage of our solitude, our scrupulous faithlessness to meaning. A queer business, truly, but our own:

> A poet could not but be gay
> In such a jocund company.

Fifty million Proustians, as they say, cannot err.

Duplicitous otherness of the text! With what binary adroitness text weaves his diabolical doubleness, enticing even the most wary reader into his web of interstices, with arachnid malevolence cunningly tapping out his coded vibrations to snare the unsuspecting. What is required is a brush with which to sweep the page clean of the fibrous entrapments of the merely readerly text, to restore the freedom of the writerly text.† *Ourselves writing:* that is what we desire: text that has

†A new broom sweeps Cleanth. L.S.-M.

yet to be concretized into rigid barriers of predetermined meaning that block off our points of entry, snip our networks, denude our languages. What we want is writing without style, structuration without structure, essay without coherent development of thought. Away with meanings! An erotics of pluralist signification is in order. Come to me, Marianne, clapped and syphilitic though you may be: perpetual present of infinite dispersion. Only you do I adore.

Very well. As I write I am resident temporarily in a community in the state of North Carolina in the United States of America, far from my friends, and leagues distant from the City of Light. Ah me. I shall beguile myself by what over here is called by some a "good read." Here is a text, which I have never seen, lying by the telephone. I pick it up at random and examine it.

Size: 9 " by 11" by 1".
Weight: ca. 1½ lbs.
Paper: cover 80 lb. enameled board. Contents 8 lb.
    newsprint, 352 pp.
Format: 18-pt. columns, sans serif capital & lower case.

Cover is bled to edge. Photograph: full color, but reddish tinge. Woman, long light brown hair, white shirt with sleeves rolled just above elbows, blue skirt, bracelet on left wrist, sandals on feet. She is walking along a brick patio, followed by a dog of medium size, brown with white paws and tail tip. The evening sun is casting both in long shadows. To her left, a brick building, very large windows with wooden panes, painted white. A flower box in front of each window. Gutter piping runs down from roof to patio alongside building. A large white glass globe is suspended from a curved iron bracket along the brickwork. Along right side of patio are areas of flowers and what appear to be railway baggage carts.

Where is the girl going? She is smiling; she seems to be strolling rather than walking briskly. She is looking to her left. What she sees there is not visible, but apparently it amuses her. There is, one senses, anticipation in her expression. The dog, by contrast, evinces no interest in or concern for what exists to the left, out of the photograph. He merely follows along behind the girl.

So? What shall I make of this text? Text gives me certain instructions, exercises his tyranny. Text bears, in addition to the photograph, certain signifiers. CHAPEL HILL AND CARRBORO, INCLUDING RESEARCH TRIANGLE PARK, it announces. And TELEPHONE DIRECTORY AREA CODE 919 NOVEMBER 1980. Aha. SOUTHERN BELL(E). What are the *lexias?* Girl is southern belle, and must be walking alongside her plantation. She is looking to the left at the happy slaves toiling at their humble tasks, even while singing "Comin' for to carry me home!" Or is it her lover who is off there? Is it a rendezvous with him toward which she strolls so amiably? There are hints: *Triangle* = delta = Venus. *Park* = trees, flowers, bushes = liaison. Are the bushes located behind the *Chapel on the Hill?* And what a strange word is *Carrboro. Car(r)* = automobile? *Boro* = burro? What can it mean? I look in my pocket dictionary: *10,000 Most Used Words, English/French.* The word does not even exist! Now one *is* curious. Immediately one thinks of the mysterious signifiers *Area Code 919.* So a code is involved. A secret code! Let us see: *919.* The number *nine:* surely the playing card. The nine of hearts? Of course: the southern bell(e)! followed by, in search of, the *one*—the ace: but, of *spades!* Could it be that . . .

Here, unfortunately, the manuscript breaks off. What would have followed we can only guess. Yours is as good as mine. L.S.-M.

Alice Kiickstand

If Anything Will Stand You Up Cold, Winter Will: Laconic Section for a February Festival

1

Suasion's sway so bloops and extrudes the be-looped
lops and shuffles flushed along any periphery's countless
coronary counter-implosions, these seasonal

seesaw-saying bells resembling salience's belly-sailings,
such the sexual elation-elongations that, before
longing's long, they're going to make everybody knock

off (knocking up, around, down; knickknacks, knockknocks,
or the laser-laze of doping off—whatever loafes and lifts
gifts of solar shrift from the niftiness or mere thrifty

sift-drift-shift nature seems to say seems, as glyphed,
nature's natural nature) to observe Archie's Birthday:
most stores'll close: need a pack of Winstons or

2

Salems (say), then the nearest 7-11 will offer you your
only retail-outlet recourse (7-come-11: a clock-configured
prime-time rhyming analog of cool good luck): the P.O.

with hoop-la of poo-bahs is going to go and come
out with its Ammons Issue, a 0¢ stamp featuring some
spherically motile likeness of something rather much

like next-to-near-nothingness's last cousin central
to the emptily perforated abundantly precancelled design,
to cost a bottom dollar plus a pretty penny or two too to

buy but be as sheer-zip zero postophallically (male mail:
see seedy parcels of seminal excitation make exits, meted
and meat-shot through breezy airs at large—let's let the jet

3

set get wet yet, pet, et cet.—or sled-sped up ringing
        womany
one-many grooves of small change: go far, Fargo): the
rooting and oratory will glooze on forever: even unevenly

mum mountains will moan monotones loft, while bigwig
        winds
(and there are witerally willions of them) unwinding will
heckle and chide or hides unhidden: hear here: and deliver

there their hideless selves of many a minimal maxim: boo:
hiss: hoo: not only will Corson's Inlet itself fill itself
uppishly up mottled o'er with mottoes and magnificent

monuments, but the w(hole) area (just to play it the
safeway: win, dixie!) the (ahem, ahaw), entire territory
from up, oh, about, say, uh, let's just let us see here

4

now, Great Egg Harbor Inlet to the north, then on down
around the thickish but withal limp crank of Cape May
        (and,

then again, May Not), on along back up over and around

the topolog-symbol of all backache and longing where New
(new!) Jersey sucks in its gut longwindedly, as much away
    awry
then as (and may the patron saint of oyster-lovers bless my

soul) Bivalve, and even over as fur piece west as Fortescue
in Cumberland Co. (106,850) will all by govt. order be
    brazenly
bronzed: what won't take bronze'll get chromed: and what

gritty residuum of resistance along some radiant gradient
can't tolerate or stand up under or to either the
bronzing or the chroming will just have to be justly

5

jacked into these here jackets (strait, prestressed,
tantrum-tempered, no brook's brothers) of
carbon-by-Ned-molybdenum steel: nor dam's or clam's

slow slam but I WHAM THAT I BAM: stasis staid: and
    thrones,
powers, dominations, Napoleons, Naders, nabobs, Namtars,
Nebuchadnezzarim, nobodaddies and mommies of the

regnant critical posse will raise all hells of praise:
hail hail; all 50 states will have to by edict adopt
the yellowlivered grim grey granulated graupel-grown

grackle as state bird: quince state bush or shrub: elmworm
state pest: blue spruce official gymnosperm: veronica
(i.e., *vera iconica*, "true image") state figwort:

[and so on for 126 more sections]

Rodney Guggenheim

Properties, Properties

If I ever enjoyed an opera I don't remember it.
What I do remember is seeing only the one—
The Barbered Bride who by I forget—
And the only thing I could stand about it (considering
I had had to pay thirteen bucks to get in
Plus sixty-five cents for a roll of opera mints—
This was the Kennedy Center for Patronizing the Arts)
The one thing I liked was this genuinely good-looking girl
Playing a boy pretending to be a girl (I forget why)
And spending two of the three acts concealed (see?)
Behind this screen. (If you see you see more than me.)
At one point in about the fourth or fifth hour
Somebody came out theatrically scratching his (?) wig
And asking tunefully, "Why is the count
So discountenanced today?" I spoke right up,
"I think I can tell you why!" The guy beside me
Said for me to shut up with his elbow.
That's thirteen dollars I won't see again.

The ballet I have let pass entirely.
Live and let live. Dance if you must dance
(Fancy dress balls are better than no balls at all),
But don't pester me with your passes and wicked witches.

If I ever read another book
It'll be because somebody is paying me to do it

More than I can make carrying these three-hundred-pound
    sacks
Of laying mash from the storeroom to the store.
(Feed and seed, feed and seed;
That's what honest people need—
Feed and seed and a decent creed.)

You have got to have the radio for the weather
And the farm news. The rest, forget.
I don't know why they call them disk jockeys
When they probably never even saw a horse up close.
May be it's jockey in the underwearical sense of the word.
I bet that's it.

The newspaper, television, and comic books are flat
    incomprehensible.
I can't make head or tail of what's going on.
The sports page is indistinguishable from the stock market:
It's dollars, options, percentages, and slumps, either way.
I did figure out one item for one crossword puzzle,
A four-letter word meaning ''excrement''—but I couldn't
    make my word fit.
Theirs started with a D. I'm still thinking about it.

What I do go for in a big way is stage plays.
There at least you have some chance to see real people
Doing real things among real objects—*properties,*
They call them. I am fond of properties, I must confess.
If a play contains both daggers and handkerchiefs
Among its properties, I honestly don't see how it can go
    wrong.
I'm bound to get a kick out of it. And (I'm not picky
Or faddish) if you can't come up with a good dagger
I'll probably be just as happy with a radish.

Mabel Arch

Since Nothing I Ever Want Is Ever Toward the Front, I Move Boxes & Cans of Stuff That Looked Like a Good Idea At the Time

& come upon a leopard
in my kitchen cupboard.

My "hello" & his "hello"
collide like plastic taxis,
head-on, nothing to nothing.

He has bad *bad* breath
& (from the look of his eyes
& interesting teeth)
murder on his mind,

but what I have on my
mind is finding a cup
big enough to take the place

of the umbrella I've lost again
because it is going to rain.

Crystal Spangler

Desire on Silhouette Lagoon: A Harleque'en Romanza

CHAPTER ONE

As the sleek motorboat slices through the aqua effervescence of Silhouette Lagoon to approach the pearly brightness of the beach, Jennifer surveys the lush scene before her with no small trepidation, and a hint of dismay creeps into her normally dulcet tone as she exclaims, ''Captain! Oh, Captain! Why are you docking here in the middle of nowhere? Is there no settlement of any sort hereabouts? I had expected . . .''

But the Captain won't say a thing! A native Georgian with an unfortunately cleft palate, he shoots a dark glance at the clearly frightened young woman from beneath his surly brow and mumbles something indistinguishable into his dark facial hair. He throws her bags on the beach. He heaves his bulk around.

Jennifer drums her small fingers rat-a-tat-tat on the hull of the shiny craft. Is it all a huge mistake, her coming here? But what else could she have done, considering the terrible fire which swept the home of her guardians (since their parents' mysterious death some twenty years ago, Jennifer and her retarded brother Lewis have been most carefully raised) killing both Aunt Lucia and Uncle Norm and destroying the entire perfect loveliness of their antebellum mansion, leaving Jennifer with only her small inheritance, her paltry background in microbiology, and the hunting lodge somewhere deep within the fastnesses of this fabled island.

"I had hoped . . ." but Jennifer's words are lost in the slap of the waves and the oddly shrill cries of the brilliant birds which wheel in the hot blue sky. Parrots and shy tropical creatures peek out at her from the shiny green leaves of the junglelike vegetation which threatens to engulf the beach; the shriek of an apparent panther is heard.

"Harg!" the Captain barks. Clearly he wants to be quit of this spot before dark, wants to be back on the mainland hefting a brew with his rustic buddies.

Jennifer mounts the dock with a sigh, traverses its rotting length, and turns to wave a reluctant farewell to the enigmatic Captain who even now is rounding the great Grey Lady rocks which mark the harbor, slipping from her view. Well.

Although she is petite and somewhat fragile in appearance, a spark of mischief in Jennifer's eye belies the seeming frailty of her frame. Actually, Jennifer is not frail at all! She's strong as an ox, and also she looks terrific when she gets dressed up. But right now she wears a lime green T-shirt, a khaki wrap-around skirt, and espadrilles. Her wispy brown locks are caught fast in a gold barrette which used to belong to her mother. Jennifer hefts the weight of her luggage and trudges through the wet unwelcoming sand across the narrow beach and up a faint trail into the very jungle, vines slowing her progress as she bites her lip to hold back her brimming tears, as night begins to fall . . .

CHAPTER TWO

Plucky Jennifer manages to set up her tent in a clearing beneath a giant live oak, where she eats a Granola bar, lights her Coleman lantern, and soon is competently ensconced in the jungle wilderness.

But suddenly we note the rustle of palm fronds, the swish of savannah grass, the warning chorus of tree frogs. Footsteps are heard on the path. Jennifer, who was very nearly asleep, stands to face the invader. Jennifer's teeth clatter helplessly in the tropic night.

"Yes?" she cries bravely into the darkness. "Yes? Who's there?"

"Rock Cliff," comes the terse reply.

"I don't believe I have had the pleasure!" Jennifer casts open the tent fly.

Light streams out to reveal the rugged virile form clad in well-worn (tight) blue jeans, cowboy boots, and an old torn Brooks Brothers shirt open almost to the waist unveiling the wealth of dark hair on the broad, muscled chest. Beneath the sable sweep of unruly hair and the decisive black line of his eyebrows, Rock Cliff's dark eyes flash fire above the prominent jut of his cheekbones. There is a touch of world-weariness in the little lines which web the marble wideness of his brow, a suggestion of tenderness and compassion which is offset by the fleshy cruel sensuality of his mouth, his strong white teeth. All his muscles bulge.

Now we are getting somewhere!

"Miss Jennifer Maidenfern?" he inquires rudely in deep masculine tones which send an unwonted tingle up Jennifer's spine.

"I beg your pardon!" she rejoins tartly.

"I received a communication from a Miss Jennifer Maidenfern not long ago, insisting that I vacate immediately the premises of Silhouette Lodge where I have been in residence for the past ten months while finishing my novel," Rock Cliff continues. "I have now vacated those premises at enormous psychological cost as I now find I am unable to complete my novel in any other surroundings. I urge you to reconsider."

It all comes back to Jennifer now. "I sent a letter to the occupant . . ." she says slowly.

"I am the occupant," states Rock Cliff.

"I see." Jennifer realizes she is in danger of losing herself in the fiery depths of his eyes. "I'm terribly sorry," she says with an effort, "but that's quite impossible. I intend to stay."

"I am independently wealthy," asserts Rock Cliff. "I will pay any amount of money to purchase Silhouette Lodge." There's a sudden unaccustomed tremor in his voice now and we can tell how much this means to him, how his life of rich-playboy decadence has left him empty and unfulfilled, how the completion of this novel will bring back his faith in himself.

Jennifer presses her trembling lips into a firm line. "Good-bye, Mr. Cliff," she says. Attempting with shaking fingers to refasten the tent fly, she stumbles over a tortoise and falls backward suddenly, upsetting the lantern. The ever-alert Rock Cliff springs forward into the tent. Quickly he lunges past the terrified young woman to right the lantern and finds himself there suddenly on the tent floor beside her shy vulnerability and sweet trembling lips which he cannot help but cover with his own. The tent fly drops silently behind him.

So I can't see a damn thing! I want to be in that tent; I want to see it all. I want to know where he puts his hands. But here I am, reading, and there they are inside that tent, black opaque shadows moving against the flap, moving and thrashing and moving until at last he emerges with a muttered oath and stumbles off into the night.

CHAPTERS THREE, FOUR, AND FIVE

are a drag. Nothing much happening here except that Jennifer finally finds Silhouette Lodge (after several wrong turns, lots of boring flora on the trail) and meets faithful Irish house-keeper Mrs. O'Reilly, an amusing old alcoholic fond of mis-quoting familiar sayings such as "Don't put all your eggs under a basset," p. 62. Mrs. O'Reilly takes a liking to Jennifer right away, fixing her a hot buttered rum, some scones, some fig preserves. Jennifer eats with interest. Mrs. O'Reilly explains the blood feud which has always existed between the Maidenfern family and the deRigeurs on the other side of the island: an insult, a slight, a missing emerald. Mrs. O'Reilly praises the exemplary conduct of the recent occupant, Mr. Cliff (Ha! Ha!), relates the complete history of Silhouette Lagoon and is working up to its geographic configurations when thank God she is interrupted by the surprise entrance of Charles Fine, the young Episcopal rector from the mainland who has sailed over in his lovely sloop "The Dove" especially to bid Jennifer welcome.

"Welcome," he smiles.

"Why, thank you," Jennifer returns.

Jennifer cannot fail to notice this young bachelor's peaches 'n' cream complexion, his lithe body, the warm sincerity of his soft blue gaze.

"If there is anything I can do to assist you," Charles Fine offers as he prepares to cast off, "anything at all . . ." His voice rings like a bell.

"I'll let you know," responds Jennifer. She watches him sail away until his boat is a mere black dot against the shimmering sea; she approves of him, Jennifer does, with all her fluttering heart, and she cannot understand the recent blush which climbed her features unawares when Mrs. O'Reilly mentioned that blackguard Rock Cliff. Oh! A hand flies up to Jennifer's mouth. It is, of course, her own.

CHAPTER SIX

Jennifer settles in. The island sun paints a glint of gold on her plain brown locks and a dusting of freckles across the bridge of her nose. One morning she's hard at work refurbishing all the furniture in the east parlor when who should arrive but Rock Cliff! Jennifer—caught barefooted, no makeup, in one of her oldest frocks—tries to flee the parlor, but he blocks her way with his muscled girth.

"Not so fast, young lady!" drawls Rock Cliff. He actually

appears to be amused; how dare he? "I've been thinking it over and I feel I owe you an apology."

"I should say so!" snaps Jennifer. And then somehow she finds herself weakening, smiling up into those eyes. She can feel his breath on her skin. He leans closer, closer, closer...

Breaking free with a momentous exercise of pure will, Jennifer evades the virile visitor and commences to wash the woodwork on the other side of the room.

"Now, Jennifer," he entreats, following her slim figure, "I want to make it up to you, Jennifer, if I may call you that. I'd like to take you out to dinner tonight."

Furiously, silently, Jennifer scrubs.

Rock Cliff edges ever closer. "Come on, now," he implores. " I feel a real connection between us, Jennifer. I sensed it from the first. I'm sorry I lost my head, but your nearness combined with the hot charm of the night..." Rock Cliff has edged so close to Jennifer that she has been forced to retreat still farther, has in fact climbed upon the windowsill itself, a precarious perch.

"Please, my dear," he begs passionately.

"I'm warning you, Rock Cliff!" shrills Jennifer, but then she tumbles—scrub brush, water pail, and all—straight onto the wide-planked cypress floor, overturning a handsome old desk, an ottoman, and Rock Cliff himself, who sprawls violently beside her in the sudden sea of suds.

Jennifer giggles infectiously. Rock Cliff catches her merriment and guffaws heartily, then turns to her with yearning eyes and clasps her wet torso firmly in his rippling arms. "My dear," he says.

"Oh, Rock," yields Jennifer, as...

CHAPTER SEVEN

"I might have known!" cries Monica deRigeur. "Look at you, Rock Cliff, down there on the floor all wet and unkempt in a compromising position!"

"Now, wait just a minute," drawls Rock.

But Jennifer sees the emerald engagement ring on Monica's tapered digit.

"No!" Jennifer leaps up and stamps her petite foot. "Don't wait at all! Just leave! Both of you! I see right through you, Rock Cliff, you and your fashionable fiancée!"

Monica, by the way, is a real bitch, wearing a low-necked blue-flowered voile dress which does nothing to hide her voluptuous form. White high-heeled sandals and a strand of priceless pearls about her swanlike neck complete the ensemble. Her upswept coiffure is elegant, implicit, or imminent, or something. I give up. "Move it, lover boy," she directs haughtily.

"This is all a terrible misunderstanding," Rock states, but the force of Jennifer's grief ejects them both from the room.

CHAPTER EIGHT

Jennifer sends for her retarded brother and adopts a wild raccoon which she names Bruce, then nicknames Posy. (?)

CHAPTER NINE

Jennifer and Lewis are sunbathing on the secluded pink shell beach when here comes Charles Fine in his nautical white sloop, ready to propose to Jennifer. "I need a helpmate," he explains earnestly, holding Jennifer tight in his strong ecclesiastical arms where she sheds a single tear upon realizing who it is she really loves.

"The cat is out of the bag now, I guess!" and, oh no, it's Rock Cliff who has been concealed behind some hydrangea bushes observing this tender scene. Rock Cliff's statement about the cat confuses Lewis, who becomes quite frightened and begins to weep openly. As Jennifer rushes to comfort her poor brother, helpful Charles Fine attempts to explain things to the irate Rock Cliff.

"You must not misconstrue . . ." Charles Fine begins.

"Misconstrue, hell!" shouts Rock Cliff, his fiery temper erupting totally since he has just broken his long-standing engagement to the beauteous Monica deRigeur only to find his dream girl in the arms of another man. Rock Cliff stalks off into the jungle just as lightning splits the summer sky and thunder rolls off the horizon, signaling the oncoming hurricane. A distraught Jennifer resists the fervent pleas of Charles Fine and Mrs. O'Reilly. She insists upon setting off immediately in search of Rock Cliff and there she goes, accompanied only by her pet raccoon, into the dark wild jungle, into the eye of the storm.

CHAPTER TEN

just goes on and on! Jennifer is lost in the swamp, buffeted by the hurricane, set upon by wild dogs, defended by Posy, and drenched to the skin. Night falls. Jennifer finally takes shelter in a cave which strangely enough turns out to contain her parents' grave (!) as well as a sealed cask holding some long complicated To Whom It May Concern letter implicating the deRigeurs in her parents' death and explaining the curse of the emerald. Who cares? Jennifer tosses and turns in a restless doze, yet feels strangely warm because of her parents' presence. At the first blush of dawn she sallies forth and retraces her steps through the jungle until she spots Silhouette Lodge at last through the dense fronds.

"Posy, we're home!" Jennifer tells the exhausted raccoon.

"And it's about time!" cries Rock Cliff, who has thought better of his hasty actions and has been scouring the jungle all night long hunting for Jennifer. The bedraggled lovers rush toward each other and meet in a passionate embrace on the pink shell beach. Their clothes are all torn and wet, revealing their contours anew in the paleness of dawn. They kiss hungrily as Mrs. O'Reilly, Lewis, and Charles Fine steal out to the edge of the beach to share this happy moment. "Well, it's an ill wind which blows nobody,'' Mrs. O'Reilly observes with a chuckle, and Charles Fine reveals that he plans to teach Lewis to sail. Rock Cliff casts the unlucky emerald into the waiting waves; Monica deRigeur flies past in her private plane, bound for New York; Posy heaves a sigh of relief; and again the lovers embrace as, behind them, the sun rises out of the sea.

And *that's it!* I shade my eyes against the brightness of this sun, the glare off the water, but in vain: all I can see is the silhouette. Jennifer and Rock have nothing, nothing left—no faces, no bodies, not to mention fear or pain or children, joy or memory or loss—nothing but these flat black shapes against the tropic sky.

"Earl"

Rhapsody in Ugly

Your blue right eye looks toward the left,
Your brown left eye looks right,
Your true blue right eye looks to the left,
While the brown left eye looks right;
So what? What difference does it make
In the darkness of the night?

Don't bother me none that your sweet thighs
Are big around as pony kegs;
Don't upset me that your sweet thighs
Might be big as pony kegs;
I never loved no woman
Just because she had nice legs.

And it don't bother me that your brother
Is a lesbian in disguise;
Don't bother me a bit that old brother Duane
Is a lesbian in disguise;
Only a fool loves a woman
On account of family ties.

You got a forty-four caliber Warner brassiere
With a double-clutching E-flat cup;
Forty-four caliber Warner brassiere,
Double-clutching E-flat cup;
You once put curlers in your hair
But the dandruff ate them up.

I took you to the freak show
At the Alamance County Fair;
I paid your way to the old freak show,
Alamance County Fair;
For once in his life the dog-faced boy
Wasn't the worst-looking creature there.

A pretty girl's spoiled rotten
And expects an expensive corsage;
Pretty girl rides in a Cadillac
And spits on a mudflap Dodge;
My woman's happy playing Bingo
In the Burlington Moose Lodge.

Your wardrobe's second and irregular;
You buy your pantyhose by the pound;
Oh second and irregular,
Pantyhose a dollar a pound;
But I'd rather pass the time with you
Than any pretty woman around.

'Cause your heart is in the right place,
Your heart is warm and big;
You're my Poland China sweetheart,
But at heart you ain't no pig;
Yes, your heart is in the right place,
Though I can't say the same for your wig.

You never were a majorette
Or homecoming beauty queen
Or a hysterical cheerleader
Or cherry festival queen;
But eighty percent of your fingernails
Are ninety-five percent clean.

The skies they are ashen and sober
And so, I might add, am I;
It's April but looks like October
And so, I might add, do I;
But rather than leave my woman
I'd curl up in the yard and die.

Bertha V. Nation Schimmelpfennig as Alice

Excerpts from
The Awkward Book of
American Literary Antidotes
Edited by Dill Eulenspickle

Cotton Mather. The New England divine Cotton Mather was a man of great and indefatigable erudition and perhaps the single most disliked person in all the colony of Massachusetts. Solomon Stoddard, who knew him, told his grandson the young Jonathan Edwards that "truly our Heavenly Father doth sometime see fit to garb His saints in robes repulsive to our eyes." Benjamin Franklin recalled that the more abandoned of the youth of early eighteenth-century Boston delighted in calling out "Cotton, Cotton, your feet smell rotten!" as Mather's carriage passed along the streets of the town. Perhaps the most incisive comment on Mather's personality is contained in a recently discovered fragment from Samuel Sewall's famous diary:

> Oct. 12, 1714. Attended Overseers meeting. Mr. Cotton Mather gave exceeding discourse upon Wonder Working Providence as exhibited in reckoning of the library fines. Afterwards went forth with Mr. [Benjamin] Colman, who pointed to Mr. Mather riding away on palfrey, saying that so seldom did one espy a

horse's arse located atop the horse. I rebuked him, yet could but laugh at the aptness of the remark.

Whittier and Holmes. The Quaker poet John Greenleaf Whittier was not noted for readiness of wit, but on at least one occasion he exhibited a deft touch with punning. It happened when he was visiting Oliver Wendell Holmes at an ancient farm that the poet-physician had purchased near Deerfield, Massachusetts. Holmes and his son Wendell, the future jurist, were showing Whittier the grounds, and they came upon an exceedingly rickety backhouse located just behind a similarly timeworn barn. "Build thee more straight the men's rooms on thy soil," the Quaker poet quipped, neatly paraphrasing one of Holmes's best-known lines. As might be expected, however, Holmes proved more than equal to the test. Moments later a rabbit bolted across the path and disappeared through a gap in the long-unpainted wall of the barn. Wendell, Jr., who had recently returned from service in the Civil War and liked to hunt, started to pursue with his shotgun, but the elder Holmes motioned him back. "Who touches the hare in yon gray shed dies like a dog! March on!" Holmes said, thereby returning Whittier's compliment.

Emerson and Bryant. At one of the dinners that James T. Fields gave for contributors to the *Atlantic Monthly* Ralph Waldo Emerson and William Cullen Bryant were seated next to each other. The opening course was oysters on the half shell. Bryant held up an oyster on his fork and remarked, "Looks just like a semi-transparent eyeball, don't it, Waldo?" To which Emerson replied, "I would say it resembles more a fringed genital."

James and Wister. Owen Wister and Henry James met in 1915, and the conversation turned to the difficulties that beset the novelist in a colony. "I'se gwine right home dis minute and hab a look-see at *De Virginyuns* agin," James said, breaking into his familiar shuffle.

Wister responded, "I beg your pardon, cher maître. Mr. Thackeray wrote *The Virginians*—plural—whereas my humble effort is entitled *The Virginian*."

James's large round eyes grew even larger and rounder. Finally regaining his wonted composure, he said orotundly, "Wal' I be a cock-eyed egg-suckin' mule, Mista Wista, I be gwine talkin' 'bout de wrong Nobbelist!"

James and Conrad. One day Henry James asked Joseph Conrad, "Joe, what do 1066, 1492, and 1848 have in common?"

Conrad, whose spoken English was nearly as poor as his written English, replied, "Not I know—I means, I not know."

"No, no, Joe," said James; "you know not."

"Okay," said Conrad, "I know not. What do have in common 1066, 1492, and 1848?"

James drew one of his deeper breaths. "They, as one might say, are, so to speak, adjacent rooms in the Warsaw Hilton."

"You know," Conrad said, "you look a lot like Benito Mussolini."

Joyce Kilmer. Someone once asked the poet Joyce Kilmer to name his favorite tree. Kilmer, who was not quite the imbecile everyone takes him for today, answered, "The popular."

Williams and Moore. At a lawn party in Tenafly, New Jersey, held shortly after the Second World War ended, William Carlos Williams and Marianne Moore were seated on a stone bench near a maze, and both were lamenting the commercialism of the literary marketplace. "By the way, Bill," Moore said after a lull in the conversation, "there is something I've always wanted to ask you. *Why* does so much depend on a red wheelbarrow?''

Williams thought for a moment. "Because," he replied, "otherwise you'd only have imaginary gardens with realtors in them."

Hemingway and Stevens. No authoritative account has ever been given of the barroom fracas in Key West in 1936 when Ernest Hemingway, apparently goaded into a fight by a very inebriated Wallace Stevens, blackened the poet's eyes. According to John Dos Passos, however, one of those present at the time was Waldo Pierce, who reported that the fight ensued after a waiter showed Stevens a snapshot of Hemingway, barechested and unshaven, proudly holding up a tiger shark. Stevens uncapped his fountain pen, scrawled the words "The Idea of Ordure at Key West," and instructed the waiter to take it over to the table where Hemingway was seated. After reading it Hemingway walked over to Stevens's table. "Too bad I don't have my camera with me," he told the poet. "Otherwise I'd take a snap of you and call it 'The Fourteenth Way of Looking at a Blackguard.' " In response Stevens threw the contents of his glass in Hemingway's face, and the fight was on.

Faulkner. When visiting New York City Faulkner tended to overindulge in alcohol as a shield against the literary life. On one occasion Bennett Cerf called for him at the Algonquin, to find him seated alone in his room, looking very morose, with a half-empty bottle of Cutty Sark on the table next to him. "Come on, Bill," Cerf said, "let's go out and get some lunch. There's a little restaurant on Forty-ninth Street that specializes in country cooking, and they're serving fresh corn-on-the-cob these days. How about it?"

Faulkner rose unsteadily to his feet and groped for his coat and hat. "Jes' call me Temple Drake," he drawled.

Nabokov and Wilson. When Edmund Wilson and Vladimir Nabokov were engaged in their public debate over the translation of Russian into English, Wilson is reported to have sent the following postcard message to Nabokov: "Scratch a Slav and you find a slob." To which Nabokov retorted, also by postcard: "Scratch a Bunny and you contract Tularemia."

"St. John Per Se"

Dusts

Translated by Bernardino Korzeniowski

I

There must be dust in every corner of the universe!

There must be dust in every corner of the universe,
   and it must say the same message to those among us
   with the power to listen,

And also to those among us without the power to listen,

And those with the will and the power to listen, as well as
   those among us with the will to listen but not the power,
   not to mention those with the power to listen but not
   the will or those among us with neither the power nor
   the will but only the memory, the mere memory, the
   recollected memory of listening,

And the burden of that oracular message in the dust is this:
There must be dust in every corner of the universe.

The dust in every corner of the universe seems as it were to
whisper the message as though in French that was then
fed automatically through a large dark ciphering
machine,

A large dark ciphering machine of the sort used by the
diplomatic corps and also used by the military services
of the land and of the sea and of the air and of
the undersea,

A very large and very dark machine for creating and
preserving ciphers by means of a keyboard with letters
which one punches with one's diplomatic or military
fingers

So that what goes in is not what comes out—that which
goes in is not the same as that which comes out, and so
that that which comes out by the same mysterious token
is not that which went in,

And the dust with its finger writes the burden of the
message of itself in the dust of itself, dust writing in
dust,

Dust that courageously and bravely resists the common
anonymity which assuetude assigns to dust,

Denying dust even the dignity of a name that is not
collective, all-inclusive, without a plural, but that which
the dust is seen to say as it writes the burden of its
message in the medium of its own self remains in essence
this: *There is dust in every corner of the universe.*

CCXVI

The message inside the message that the element of dust
    writes as a burden by means of the fingers of itself in the
    medium of itself is not so much *dust* as *dusts,*

Dusts in the plural as though with variation, difference,
    change, multiplicity, personality, and names,

Many names!

What idiot got it into his head that dust ought to be
    anonymous! No! Oh, no! Dust is not anonymous! Dust
    is onymous!

O onymous dust: forgive us for paying so little attention to
    you in your manifold manifestations in every corner of
    the universe,

Some of which we may ourselves in time surely and certainly
    become! O onymous dusts!

Your names O dust are legion and I now call you Legion!
    Your names are Julius and Alexander, Napoleon and
    Frederick, Grant and Thompson, Marmaduke Pickthall
    and the Coventry Master!

O dusts in every corner of the universe! O Walt and
    Stéphane and Ezra and Thomas and Hart! O ageless and
    everlasting dusts, I could go on and on and on,

On and on and on, I say, so as to seem to go on forever and
    ever!

Judi Pêché

Laser Tacos

This here is an old song which I learned from my mama's papa
in Pittsylvania County, Virginia—the place used to be called
Motley, between Sycamore and Hurt—and which goes back
into the common science-fiction food-lore in Indo-European
pre-history and (indexed as motif 1377.3, *Quest for the
hazelnuts of ay, ay, ay*) finds parallels and analogues in the
culinary thorn rhapsodies of Central Africa, the yam sagas of
Polynesia, and chow-totem epic of Australia, the longest word
in Aristophanes, and certain Native American barbecue festi-
vals.

You don't see certain products or brand names any more
'Cause things just aren't the way they were down at the
corner store,
    Ipana and Studebaker
    Have gone to meet their Maker,
And the stuff we eat's fantastic to the core.

(We now eat)   LASER TACOS
(Yes I said)   LASER TACOS
    Where Captain Kirk is Colonel Saunders' boss,
(Come get your)   LASER TACOS
(Old-fashioned)   LASER TACOS
(Yeh!)   LASER TACOS
                    with the
                    radioactive sauce.

The Pope now runs communion bread through a
     microwaving toaster,
He's got a motor-driven rosary for a high-speed "Pater
     Noster,"
Studebaker and Ipana
Have sailed to their Nirvana
With Jamie Summers on a big bionic poster.

               LASER TACOS
               LASER TACOS
They're the greatest invention since Noah built his ark
               LASER TACOS
               LASER TACOS
Throw away your lights 'cause these jewels glow in the dark.

     They're a big fad now in Texas
       And all across the South—
     Just like a Roller Derby
       Inside your very own mouth!

Take you a tortilla made of Teflon . . . Cooked in Lincoln
Zephyr grease . . . Then fold it down the middle . . . With a
parabolic crease . . . Put a cubic centimeter . . . Of lasers—that
stands for Light Amplification by Stimulated Emission of
Radiation—on your intergalactic cheese and some Darth
Vader lettuce and just a soupcan of evangelical pentecostal
apocalyptic tabernacle double-clutching Old Durango
magnum-force born-again Leviticus & Deuteronomy
E-flat-major towering inferno chili powder with one whole
wild onion of Borneo, some automatic tomatoes grown on
the grave of a dragon, and a little anti-matter
dilithium-crystal million-Roentgen sauce—and what you
got?

(Well you got)   LASER TACOS
(Woo woo woo)   LASER TACOS
    The hint of a whiff might drive you out of your mind
('Cause they're called) LASER TACOS
(Oh, Lordy)   LASER TACOS—
    It's a close encounter of the seventy-seventh kind.

Iowa Olive

Variations on a Theme by Betsy Bell

If when dialing your own long distance call
A wrong number you should befall
Secure the number that you have obtained
Dial 'O' for the operator and to her explain.
      "Betsy Bell Says," Bell Telephone Company

1

When to the sessions of sweet silent thought
I summon up remembrance of things past,
I sigh the lack of many a thing forgot,
And with old woes new wail my dear time's waste:
'Tis then I dial direct to far friends' houses
And o'er the phone relive my old carouses.

2

Shall I, wasting in despair,
Die for lack of airplane fare?
Or make pale cheeks with care
'Cause my budget's spread too rare?
Be she farther than a day,
Or vacationing at Cape May,
    With my telephone close to me
    What care I how far she be?

3

So smooth, so sweet, so silvery is thy voice
As, could they hear, the damned would make no noise,
But listen to thee (thy phone shall by thy lyre)
Melting melodious words and copper wire.

4

Yet once more, O ye dial tones, and once more,
Ye party lines, with busy signal drear
I come to verify an area code,
And crowded circuits load,
By calling at the busiest time of year.

5

When lovely woman stoops to marriage
And finds too late that men betray,
What charm can vanquish baby carriage,
What art can wash the tears away?

The only art her bills to cover
Is, in a court of law to seek

Remittance from her onetime lover,
And call her mother once a week.

6

Ring out, phone bells, to the wild sky,
   The flying cloud, the frosty light:
   The year is dying in the night;
Ring out, phone bells, and let him die.
Ring out the old, nor ring collect;
   Ring, happy bells, and never slumber:
   The area code, and then the number.
'Tis cheaper if you dial direct.

7

Sing on there in the hallway
O telephone bashful and tender, I hear your notes,
   I hear your call,
I hear, I come presently, I understand you,
But for a moment I linger, so be not impatient,
Ring for a full half-minute or more before you
   hang up,
Delaying not, hurrying not.

8

Now that we're almost settled in our house
I'll call the friends that cannot sup with us
Beside our wood stove in the library,
And having talked transcontinentally
Climb up the brand-new carpeted stairs to sleep:
'Tis good to speak of ancient truth
With boon companions of one's youth,
And after five p.m. the rates are cheap.

79

9

Time and the bell have buried the day,
The black cloud carries the sun away.
If you need help to make your call,
Dial 'O' and we will do it all.

10

Whose woods these are I think I know.
His house is in the Village though;
He will not see me dialing here
The darkest evening of the year.
The woods are lovely, dark and deep,
But I have promises to keep
And would have been marooned for ages—
It pays to use the Yellow Pages.

L'envoi

Mordecai, Mordecai, Mordecai Brown!*
How come you goin' aroun' and aroun'?
"I heard the Yellow Pages talking:
'Let your fingers do the walking.' "

*Mordecai "Three-Finger" Brown, also known as "Miner,"
  famous pitcher for the Chicago Cubs of the 1900s and
  1910s.

A Selection from
THE
NORON
READER

A Multicultural Wholistic
All-Purpose ''Reader'' for
''Readers'' of All Ages
Who're No Morons!
Edited by Loch Leman

Poetry

Considering him/her in the general overarching context in terms of nineteenth-century American literature, culture, socioeconomic development, science, and technology terms, Emily Dickinson was rather unique in being immortalized today in terms of an analyzation of life-style and sexual preferences on the stage in the form of a theatrical drama including a television version on educational television opposite celebrity bowling which was a success of esteem if not an all-time knockout, rating-wise. Ms. Dickinson wrote the whole long poem from which the following excerpt is excerpted probably sometime between the years 1830 and 1886, when she was born and dead but not published until later, which all of her poems except for 7 out of approximately 1775 were. Being as she lived in the olden days not typing and short of paper, the poem has no title in the sense of being entitled but we think you will agree with us, that it nevertheless is quite a real POEM (see *Glossary,* s.v. "CREATIVE WRITING, FORMS OF"). Without farther adieu then hear it is ready or not.

Untitled Poem (first verse)

I taste a liquor never brewed[1]
From tankards scooped in pearl,
Not all the vats[2] along the Rhine
Yield such an alcohol.[3]

1. Of course no liquor is ever brewed in the scientific sense, beer is brewed. If Ms. Dickinson had said, "I taste a beer never brewed" that would be a PARADOX (see *Glossary*), but the statement as it stands is simply a mistake of fact, like

saying, "I read a book never written," which is absurd (see *Glossary*, s.v. ALCOHOLISM OF THE ABSURD) (for what "s.v." means, also see *Glossary*, s.v. ENIGMATIC ABBREVIATIONS, UTILIZATION AND/OR USAGE OF). The "I" in Ms. Dickinson's touching tautology is not of course Ms. Dickinson herself but the PERSONNA (see *Glossary*, s.v. BLADES) of the poem.

2. Wrong! While liquor is not brewed, it is particularly not brewed in vats which beer is. Ms. Dickinson probably meant "still" in the somewhat unique sense in which it was employed by the well-known famous author T. S. Eliot in the line "At the still, point of the turning world/etc."

3. Harvard and other researchers have tabulated for computer-processing purposes the number of times Ms. Dickinson alluded to beer, wine, liquor, and anodynes in her great poems and the count is staggering. (See also *Glossary*, s.v. WHY WRITERS BOOZE IT UP SO MUCH.)

QUESTIONS FOR DISCUSSION ON
THE WORLD AND FARTHER STUDY
(MULTIPURPOSE)

I Creative Writing

Looking into your heart, a poem could be written on self-expression in terms of what Ms. Dickinson says without the onus of rhyme unless you think pearl and alcohol rhyme, in which case you do not belong in a creative-writing class but, a clinic for the DEAF. No, that's a joke, but seriously you too— esp. if your immature, retarded, psychotic, senile, iliterate, and want to make a lot of money in your spare time—can write just as good a poem as Ms. Dickinson with no ANXIETY or LABOR whatever, simple and direct, smooth flowing and straightforward, just by asking yourself, "What do I feel?" and "How can I express what I feel in words?" When you do that, you have already done the CREATIVE part of the process! The rest is just finding the words to externalize what is already there inside you, genuine, sincere, authentic, personal, emotional; & what teacher has the right to tell you that he/she feels you have not truely expressed your self? Express your feelings in words of your own choosing and forget about being told by some unpublished and unevolved bureaucrat you have relied maybe a bit too much, for an amateur, on BANALITY, CLICHE, SENTIMENTAL STEREOTYPES, IMITATION, DERIVATION, SUBURBAN RHYTHMS, SUPERSTITION, and a TYPEWRITER RIBBON MORE EXPERIENCED THAN YOU ARE.

Being an art form, however, you may have to "prime the pump" a little by having some kind buddy suggest his/her suggestions for how to start, you may start by correcting Ms. Dickinson's errors of fact and rhetoric, i.e.

I taste a liquor never distilled

and see where that takes you, just be sure your getting taken somewhere.

Other students have learned alot, by trying a PARODY which brings out the skeletal essence of a poem, without tampering or tinkering with it's spirit. A well-known famous author has actually published a poem, that does something of this type:

I quaff a Pepsi never bottled
In Billy the Kid, Oklahoma.
The Zip code, no, I know it not
But wish I could remember.

II *Women Studies*

Although writing in excess of 1750 poems, society in effect, raped Ms. Dickinson by accepting less than 1% for publication in refereed journals with national circulation and prestige. Have a discussion on your perceptions in terms of whether you feel she should have done something different to succeed in the white man's world. Do you agree success is counted sweetest by those who near succeed?

III Curriculum in Alcoholism and Other Addictions

Harvard and other famous researchers on a National Science Foundation "Argo" Grant have conducted interviews and questionnaires with all the bartenders in Amherst, Mass., and none of them can remember her, but there was a Dickinson woman hung out quite alot in the Brass Rail and both Pink Flamingoes until one of them burned down due to Bananas Foster in 1949. Bananas is now doing ten to twenty in soso security kraal at Chicopee. His real name is Raymond.

IV American Studies

Now, without finding out a lot of facts and stuff in the library or even in your own life, just kind of *think about* what you hear Ms. Dickinson is saying in her novel. And just kind of think about what it all *means* in terms of basic structures in the American character, and what about the all-time record-breaking consumption of alcohol in this country reaching a peak in 1830 the year he/she was born? How old do you compute Edgar Alen Poe to have been in 1830 and, so what? How old do you think you were in terms of 1830? How come? Now, without going into a lot of dry as dust detail and stuff, what makes this country what it is? Is there national character or a sort that can be isolated and judged and studied? What is the evidence for this isolation and study? Other than your accidental visceral twitchings? If you answered "Nothing," you are right and may now proceed to the next curriculum in weary stale flat, and unprofitable uses.

V Interdisciplinary study for the Consideration of Human Values Etc.

In terms of human values and philosophical attachment of value to some entity, have a discussion on your perception of whether other people feel there is some value in poetry per se, not just the reading or study thereof? We mean, uh, what we mean to say, suggest, here, is basically, uh, that you can get alot of real good, uh, experience, you know, from, out of, uh, sitting around, like on the floor of the, uh, Aquinas Center, places like that (never mind who they named the Center after, he wrote alot, we mean *alot,* of stuff and in Latin too and weighed about 200 kilos and said it was all straw anyway, okay?), and, uh, just kind of let it flow, like, over you in terms of basic, you know, we mean you know, values, not so much prices as such per uh se but in-depth stuff like uh permanence and interpreting in terms of your own interpretation valid in and uh of itself, like, what Ms. Dickinson means or rather meant, it being she wrote long ago in the olden days now no uh longer relevant exactly to our modern world's life-style?

VI Program in Myth, Religion, Divinity, and Theology

A later segment of this novel under discussion alludes or makes mention of seraphs and saints doing something. How many syllables are there in seraph? How many letters? Do you prefer *seraphs* or *seraphim* as a plural, as it were? A recent poll funded by the Franciscan Task Force for the Study of Theological Attitudes and In-Depth Thinking about Stuff found that, of 31 famous theologians polled in the poll, 29 had no preference to speak of. That, kiddo, is a whopping 93.548387%! With an average annual salary of just over $51,000 (before taxes) (after taxes too, for that matter), that comes within $21,000 of our goal of $1.5 million. Chicken-feed, sure, but you know what OT hermeneutics teaches: ''For want *of* feed a chicken *was* lost; for want *of* a chicken, a coop *was* lost; and who under the sun knoweth *where* such *things* will stop?''

Ms. D.'s College Diary—Aetat. 150

The Soul selects her own Sorority—
Then—shuts the Dorm—
From her elite Majority
Black balls—eclectic—swarm—

*

To make a Semester it takes a pizza and one B,
One pizza, and a B,
And a liberal drop-add Policy.
The policy alone will do,
If B's are few.

*

A Transcript one cannot contain
May yet a Transcript be—
Though God forbid it lift the lid—
On one's wee SAT!

*

A Diagram—of Rapture!
A sixpence at a Show—
With Holy Ghosts in Cages!
Universities would go!

*

I cannot dance upon my Toes—
No Man instructed me—
But oftentimes, among my mind,
A Glee Club tickleth me.

*

These are the Nights that Beatles love—

*

A. Murdoch—clawed my Gown—
Not *Murdoch's*—blame—

But *mine*—
Who went too near
To Murdoch's *Den*—

*

I tried to think a lonelier Thing
Than any I had seen—
Some Polar Expiation—An Omen in the Bone
Of Last Year's cute Prom Queen—

*

To own a Buick of my own
Is of itself a Bliss—
Whatever Privilege is lost, Lord,
Continue me in this!

*

Homecoming comes—Mount Holyoke
Elects home *Royalty*—
Complexion—Orthodontics—but
She can't cook good—like me.

*

Fortitude incarnate
Here is laid away
In the swift Partitions
Of the awful C—

*

In Lesbos—far—such gay Folk dwell—
None—I'll have—*None*—of them—
Mint—Kitchen—my Neutrality—
Keyless—my Diadem.

*

I drink a liquor scarcely brewed—
From Tankards etched in Greek—
I open up my Mouth—anon—
To speak—I—can—*Not*—speak—

I dwell in Delta Epsilon—
A fairer House—than yours—
No Footprints—on the windowsills—
No mirrors—on the Doors—

I dropped out—Homesick—ere the Term
Her normal Term—achieved—
My Roommate wept—sore woebegone—
Secretly relieved.

———

E. D. Back in Massachusetts

Exacerbating Character—
Standing—but for Nought—
Nor Name—nor Number—No—
Puts Proxy—in a Pout—

There blossoms a Corps of Esaus—
Whole Guilds of Gusses—wax—
Great Galaxy—the Kennedys—
Wide wondrous World of Joes—

X only will Not tell his Tale—
No—not one Dot he leaks—
Anonymous Nonentity
Evaporating quick—

Like Bedford near to Medford—
As Nap acts Aunt to Angst—
So treads—her Beat—my Heart
From Bethlehem—to Bad—

The World is Cash and Carry—
I am—a Credit Card—
The World all Cable—Color—
Mere black and white—my Set.

All-Purpose Glossary:

A Chrestomathy

Alcoholism of the Absurd. On a doctoral examination for an Ed.D. in K-12 musicology, a slow-witted candidate was asked to name, in order, the operas making up Wagner's *Ring.* Since the only musical Wagner he had ever heard of was Porter W., an underweight has-been, the candidate was silent. At last, a sympathetic examiner coaxed him: "For the first opera of the cycle, think of a beer." The candidate said, "Thanks, the answer was on the tip of my tongue: *Falstaff.*" He was told to try again. He said, *"Luisa Miller Lite?"* Close, again, but no cigar. *"La Bohème Nationale?"* On it went, until all adjourned to a nearby saloon for many quarts of Tannhäuser Busch.

Paradox. A morbid trope which denies that a thing is itself or asserts that a thing is its opposite. Patent nonsense leading to folly. If a certain nameless poet really believed that "the child is father of the man," is it any wonder that he fathered, willy-nilly, an illegitimate child? Also a favorite device in botanical nomenclature, whereby, e.g., the tulip poplar and Jerusalem artichoke have no connection with the tulip, the poplar, the artichoke, or Jerusalem. "Rare earths," likewise, are neither rare nor earths. Like the Holy Roman Empire, this kind of stuff can drive you nuts. The idea that such a stupid gimmick could be what certain fashionable Germans call the *Torquequelle* ("twistwell") of poetry is (*pace* Brooks, Empson, etc.) all wet.

J. Parkhurst Schimmelpfennig as Lear

Mordred Anatol Penguin

Literary Questions And Answers

Q. Please give the absolute lowdown on "The Waste Land." Was it written by T. S. Eliot, as I was told in college, or by Ezra Pound, as I have recently heard? Also, what do the three words at the end mean?

A. "The Waste Land" was written by Eliot while visiting the catacombs in Rome, on vacation from his job as an undertaker for Lloyds of London. Submitted to Pound for editing, it was reduced in length from eight sections to five, the unused portions being later published as "Old Possum's Book of Practical Cats." The meaning of the last line, which consists of the word "Chauncey" thrice repeated, is generally considered to be an allusion to one of the poet's Boston forebears, the Rev. Charles Chauncy (1705–1787), and refers to a blessing Chauncy once gave for a small boy who was drowned in a frog pond. Incidentally, it is of interest that it was Chauncy's blessing that later inspired Edgar Allan Poe to refer to Boston as "Frogpondia" (see Eliot's autobiographical memoir, "From Poe to Valerie.")

Q. What process did William Jennings Bryan go through to produce "Thanatopsis"?

A. It just growed.

Q. I've always been confused by why there is a Samuel Taylor Coleridge and also a Samuel Coleridge Taylor and why isn't *Biographia Literaria* called *Autobiographia Literaria?* I mean, you know.

A. You'd better re-phrase the question.

Q. Did anybody ever try to literally sing *The Song of Hiawatha?*

A. Samuel Coleridge Taylor *tried.*

Q. Recently in reading literary criticism I have encountered a number of terms that I have never seen before, such as "clinamen," "tessera," "kenosis," and "askesis." Can you tell me anything about them? What is your opinion of their efficacy?

A. The terms you refer to all come from a book entitled *The Influence of Anxiety: or, The Well-Wrought-Urn-Burial*, by Stoom Blephen, believed to be a *nom de plume* of the Irish writer James Joyce. In this connection, see the comment by Stephen Dedalus in *A Portrait of the Artist as a Young Man:* "Keep your Agon. If we must have an Artistotle, let us have a legitimate Aristotle."

Q. What did Walt Whitman mean by the "body electric"? I mean . . . you know . . .

A. The "body electric" for Whitman meant AC and DC, the latter more so than the former. His irksome habit of getting into bed between honeymooners finally got him into such hot water that he had to move to New Jersey. He once told Edward Carpenter that there was no market for heterosexual art unless it was so kinky it would turn your stomach. He cited Swinburne and Wilde, who cited him back, with interest. You know how those people are.

Q. How come, of her 1776 poems, only seven of Emily Dickinson's poems were published in her lifetime?

A. The other 1769 simply weren't good enough. The ungrammatical ravings of a virgin poised shakily between half-consonance and half-assonance will never catch on.

The Johnson versions of her poems are things written by Prof. Johnson himself—a forging perpetrated for the purpose of winning him permanent tenure at the Lawrenceville School.

Q. How many Poes does it take to screw in a light bulb?

A. Three: Edgar and Virginia to do the actual screwing and a *Tertium Quid* to accuse Longfellow of plagiarizing "Eldorado" from the Cadillac Indians of Lower Michigan.

Q. Did Robert Browning really write a poem called "The Loss Leader"?

A. He sure did. It has to do with the A&P's practice of selling sugar for less than cost to make you buy coffee for more than reasonable. Browning thought the A&P an abomination, the work of Chinamen, yellow peril one and all. One of his attacks begins, "I am poor brother Li Po, by your leave" (not to be confused with the obscure southern journalist Lee Poe).

Q. Give, in no more than a few sentences, the plot of *Paradise Lost*.

A. An author is seated in his living room reading one night, when there is a knock at the window. When he opens it a parrot enters and perches itself on the bust of the author's girlfriend, Grishkin. Though questioned repeatedly, the only thing the parrot will say is the single word "Amontillado." This goes on for a while, until there is another knock, this time at the front door, and the visitor this time is the Lady Madeline of Usher, who was by error interred some days before. The author does not like this, and flees aghast, followed by Grishkin and the parrot. As they cross the driveway a bolt of lightning strikes the house (this was before the invention of lightning rods), and all is consummated. As the curtain goes down the parrot is heard to croak, "John J. McGraw! John J. McGraw! Fetch aft the rum, John J.!" to which the author's girlfriend answers, "I see you changed your brand." The poem is eighteen stanzas, and was written by Allen Tate.

Q. Why did Billy Budd stutter?

A. A common misconception. Both Bartleby and Billy are actually Chinese Buddhist monks practicing a kind of Kung Fu quietism. Billy is not stuttering: he's speaking Chinese, which sounds like stuttering because no Chinaman ever had the fundamental imagination to invent a word of more than one syllable. I Hsi Ma El, another famous Chinaman, narrates *Moby-Dick,* which has to do with a Cantonese whale who resents the fad, circa 1850, in Fluke Fu Yung. ("Fu Yung" means "hibiscus," and Ahab was the last fancier of it before a strange lady called Ma Jong came along. She is not really Chinese.)

Q. What do Henry Adams, Henry James, Henry Longfellow, and Henry Thoreau have in common?

A. Not a damned thing I know of.

Q. Did Samuel Clemens know as much about the Mississippi River as a goose knows about geometry?

A. No.

Q. What is the difference between Henry James and William James?

A. One was a dear old queen and one wasn't. (That remark, usually attributed to General Grant, was actually originated by Pope Leo XIII, who thought John Deere was a kiss-off letter received by a jilted serviceman.)

Q. Can you explain the principles of Structuralism to me, especially as regarding literature.

A. Literary structuralism is based on the premise that the literary text is written in a code. The task of the reader is to crack the code. Using for his manual of code-breaking a copy of a short story, "Zarathustra," by Honoré de Balzac, the reader is guided by the discovery that human discourse is by nature Yaleish rather than Harvardian, as proved by the research of William Lyon Phelps, Breuer-Freud, and Edgar A. Guest, and also by the well-known fact that the most commonly used letters of the alphabet, in order of frequency, are h-i-l-l-i-s m-i-l-l-e-r. When the reader succeeds in cracking the code, he discovers that Cleanth Brooks and Robert Penn Warren have retired and the American middle class is doomed.

Q. Is it true that the playwright George Bernard Shaw did not sleep with his wife?

A. It depends in part on what is meant by "sleep." Shaw's wife, known to her friends as Saint Joan, was a very religious woman, and it is believed that the marriage was, in the technical sense, without formal carnal concupiscence. Some authorities, however, disagree, contending that it was all a dirty rumor started by Lady Astor.

Q. Quick: is *Vanity Fair* a magazine or a novel by Thackeray?

A. Yes. What is more, *House Beautiful* is another magazine whose name comes from *Pilgrim's Progress*.

Q. Once and for all: was Joyce Kilmer a man or a woman? If not, why not? And if so, why was he and/or she named Joyce?

A. Take it easy, Greasy: you got a long way to slide! Listen: Joyce Kilmer, Lou Wallace, Joyce Cary, Evelyn Waugh, Estes Kefauver, Babe Ruth, Michael Strange, and Pete Rose Magruder were all women. Some dressed up as men (which is called travesty or transvestitism or L'Eggs Across the Sea) and hit a lot of home runs as compensation. But don't be fooled: *Herself Observed*, like *The Portrait of a Lady*, is autobiographical.

Q. Why do we say "Lord Byron," but "Alfred, Lord Tennyson"?

A. The British have *never* figured this sort of thing out, and if you ask me, they never will, given constitutional limitations on their I.Q. The thing is, though, that Byron's name was George Noel Gordon, Baron Byron (i.e., the family name was not the same as the title of nobility and nobody is going to call a pugnacious hypersensitive millionaire genius and beauty "Baron Byron" to his face more than once) while Tennyson was *made* a baron *de novo* but not *ab ovo,* if you can see the difference, so that his name and his title were the same, so there's no need to say something echoic like "Alfred Tennyson, Lord Tennyson" or "first Baron (of) Tennyson." If you can handle an analogy that's been in place since 1057, it's like the practice with cardinals: the title comes between the first name and last name, as in Red Cardinal Schoendienst.

Q. What was the slam dunk called before Abner Doubleday invented basketball?

A. The Last Daze of Pompey's Head.

Book Review Section

Reviewed by Grogan Furfur Pitt

Poor Tom's A-Cold

Great Tom: Notes towards the Definition of T. S. Eliot by T. S. Matthews (Harper and Row, 1974. 210 pages. $8.95)

Of the internationally celebrated journalist and biographaster T. S. Matthews, Esq., we know but little at first hand apart from the few meagre bits of information that he has let slip either deliberately or inadvertently. Or, indeed, misinformation: he did, after all, exchange his native American's birthright of "straight talk" for that superfoetation of anfractuous pottage called *Time.*

We know, to take a simple if pungent example, what

"T. S." stands for. (The Americans would say "runs for.")
Matthews dwelt awhile in the centre of London (probably the
one in Great Britain, but just possibly the one in Ontario:
these journalists' stock in trade is, after all, a species of fictive
ingenuity that approaches fraud). We know, furthermore,
that he was married (or perhaps—such speculations and hy-
potheses are not forbidden—joined by the instrument of some
rather less formal espousal or liaison) to a British (or, at any
rate, *ostensibly* British) woman (or, in any event, woman *à
rebours*—in the idiom once characterised as the "Timethod"
by James Thurber, the late wit, what one might denominate a
"womanqué"). And we know, if we permit our imaginations
to expand amongst the possibilities with the exuberance that
Blake identified with Beauty, that he may have been the
semilegendary Piper's Son against whom a charge of swine
theft was brought in 1934 but later dropped when the *corpus*
(or, more precisely, *porcus!*) *delicti* could not be produced in
court by one Tom Sawyer, the feckless bailiff who may or may
not play a role in a curious—nay, extraordinary—book by
Matthews entitled *Great Tom*. (If greater bibliographical
detail is desired, the reader may consult a genuinely solid
piece by a Mr. Guttikonde Nageswara Rao, M.A., in that
perfectly enchanting Bombay periodical, the *Aryan Path,* Vol.
XXXVIII, No. 1, pp. 266–71.)

To pursue these jugs of inviolable publicity, we need what
was once called "hard work" by Mr. John Mize, a silly-mid-on
for a professional baseball organization. (Mr. Mize has now
become one of the "boys" in the sense intended by Mr.
Graves in his poem that begins, "I see the boys of Sumer in
the ruins.") By some diligence and the kind of sedulous
archaeology of the imagination alien to the layman but all in a
day's work to the ambitious journalist-in-exile, we can ascer-
tain that Matthews, at the age of sixty-eight, stopped smoking. Or rather, that is to say that *he says* he stopped. But, of
course, the overwhelming question remains unanswered:

stopped . . . smoking . . . *what?* In the text that forms the basis of our scrutiny and guesswork here, he quite simply *does not say.* Not in so many words. The combustible material being consumed is not unambiguously specified.

Now, as one must recognize, the innocent reader may balk at this point and object that when a modern man claims to have stopped smoking he means smoking tobacco products or (if he be what the French, with their natural Mediterranean gift for apt epithets, call *un Américain*) just possibly odd lengths of grapevine. Pressing this problem of enquiry to its next logical steppe, we may remember that the *Grapevine* is the periodical of Alcoholics Anonymous, so that a supposition that Matthews is in all probability a tragically heavy drinker is by no means out of the question or beyond the limits of bio-journalistic courtesy. And, should that strike the innocent researcher as either farfetched or unkind, then a decent compromise may be easily found, to wit: what Matthews stopped smoking at the age of sixty-eight was vodka. And, if not that, what? Cubebs have gone the way of all flesh.

Flesh! DA! *There* (as King Lear might be stimulated to exclaim) is the rub! Flesh: and flesh (as Eliot rather clumsily adumbrates in the fortunately abandoned *Coriolan* torso) is grass. I daresay that what Matthews stopped smoking was larkspur. An authentically haunting phrase from the foreigner Lorca, whom Matthews is beyond any shadow of a doubt old enough to have known *quite* intimately, seems apposite: *las criaturas en carne viva.* Since we have substantially corroborative grounds to suspect strongly that Matthews is fully familiar with speakers of the Spanish persuasion, it is most difficult to accept any proposition except the natural, logical, and Anglo-Catholic explanation concerning these "creatures in living flesh." Over and above the larkspur already alluded to, Matthews smoked scorpions. (Whoever wrote *Hurry Up Please it's Newsweek* on the wall of the W.C. in my local is, by the way, all wet.)

What else might one conclude about Matthews? What else, that is, in the absence of any firsthand information or sympathetic insight? Did he wear clothing? Inveterately. Did he serve his time at the altar of the rite of Onan? Indubitably. Did the tyres of his Humber Super-Snipe ever scrape against a kerb of Edgeware Road? Undeniably. This is easy! (Sometimes, lost in a shaft of sunlight or something, we think we know what Manning meant. What is the "nice flop of deg" that Northern Farmers admire so much?)

Tracking down Matthew's religion is no easy matter, although he himself admits to having become at one time an Anglo-Catholic. Our best course here will be to examine the parallel testimony of a very great man indeed who, by one of those queer freaks of fortune, was both an Anglo and a Catholic. I am referring, of course, to John Henry ("Cardinal") Newman, and his affidavit is to be found in that admirable little treatise, *An Essay in Aid of a Grammar of Assent.* "I have meant to say," he says there, " 'I am a Catholic, for the reason that I am not an Atheist.' This makes the misinterpretation of my words which I am exposing the more striking, for it paraphrases me into a threat and nothing else, viz., 'If you are not a Catholic, you must be an Atheist, and will go to hell.' Mr. Lilly, in his letter in my defence, sees this, and most happily adopts the positive interpretation which is the true one." If those strong words leave us yet in the dark as regards Matthews's religion, a further sentence from Newman should do the job: "Religion has, as such, certain definite belongings and surroundings, and it calls for what Aristotle would call $\pi\epsilon\pi\alpha\iota\delta\epsilon\upsilon\mu\acute{\epsilon}\nu os$ investigator, and a process of investigation *sui similis.*" That clinches it!

So "Tom" Matthews is formulated. There is nothing else that wants adding, unless it be a few citations of verse from that other "Tom" whom the world knew as T. S. Eliot. Can one adduce as further evidence of his essential Christadelphianism some lines from Eliot's "Triumphal March," with which Matthews was most certainly capable of making himself completely familiar: "Don't throw away that sausage, / It'll come in handy"? One can scarcely ignore the original beginning of "The Burial of the Dead," which goes quite a long way in elucidating and even enodating the roots of April's superlative cruelty: "Old Tom, boiled to the eyes, blind." (Here April is really, like the "depraved May" in "Gerontion," a woman and not a month. The same May is told "goonight" at the end of "A Game of Chess." Good old Depraved May... Blown, I reckon, to bits by now. But I digress.) And what about these words of the First Tempter in *Murder in the Cathedral:* "Old Tom, gay Tom"?

But we must come to a stop. At a certain point, such probing for the meaning, the secret plurisignations—of T. S. becomes a waste. It isn't Tristram Shantih. Or Trafalgar Square. Or Turkey Shoot.

Ralph Lying Bull

A Leaf from Wretched Richard's Almanac

Review of *Mid-Thigh Was My Nightie* by Carolyn Czar (1971)

Not, of course, so much the metaphysics of masculinity as (*mutatis mutandis,* needless to say) the actual or prophetic masculinity of metaphysics—in the sense of *meta* the *Physics* in the grand but fluked *Organon* attributed to the Hellenistic generation of Poet-critic-marine-biologists usually, if inaccurately, subsumed under the denomination "Aristotle"—is, let us say at least provisionally if not as authoritatively as the example and pathos of Richard Blackmur would warrant, what Miss Czar, long recognized as our own not peculiar but at any rate idiosyncratic American alembic's mixture of Semiramis and Mrs. Eddy, repudiates and, paradoxically, simultaneously *with the same grandly endowed hand,* embraces in a pacific (lower case!) catholic (O! O! lower case again!) fashion— however unfashionable—that can hardly (in justice, or *tendresse,* either, for that matter, if, indeed, matter it be, so intellectually does it appropriate the fervid *mousse* of both its ardors and initiatives) be said, be read to dismiss: dis-miss, at least in the Roman (. . . *nunc* . . .) ambiance of that honored rubric.

Explored more expansively (did not Ezra Pound insist on making it new, even while the book with that title consisted only of old essays?), the patent point exposes, as though petal by petal, the muscle of the heart as well as the warmth, the biodegradable immediacy of the literal mind as one is recycled once more through the crepuscular parameters of what martyrs call American life today, life being, as any sensitive ear could, if attuned, decoct, an irony of ironies, given the current decay of what we once could call language.

Letters to the Editor

SIR,

The editorial in your last issue, "We Must Not Forget History," signed with the initials "J.P.S.," which I presume are those of the editor, contains several factual errors about American history and literature.

The owner of the cow that supposedly kicked over a lantern and started the Chicago fire of 1873 was a Mrs. O'Leary, not Elsie Borden.

Admiral David Glasgow Farragut's famous remark at the Battle of Mobile Bay in 1864 was made in reference to Confederate mines placed in the ship channel, and not to the unhealthy climate of the Gulf Coast area. What he is quoted as having said is not "Damn the mosquitoes!" but "Damn the torpedoes! Full speed ahead!"

The inventor of the process for readying rubber for domestic use by vulcanization was Charles Goodyear, not Henry J. Trojan.

The name of the frog in Mark Twain's sketch "The Celebrated Jumping Frog of Calaveras County" is Daniel Webster, not Kermit.

The so-called "Boston Massacre" took place on King Street near the State House, not at Fenway Park, and soldiers of the British Army, not the New York Yankees, were involved.

The celebrated remark "I propose to fight it out along this line if it takes all summer" was made by Major General U. S. Grant, not Alexander Graham Bell.

The initial that Hester Prynne wears on her bosom in Nathaniel Hawthorne's *The Scarlet Letter* is an "A," not an "F."

The Indian tribe whose representatives sold Manhattan Island to the Dutch in 1836 was known as the Canarsies, not the Shmohawks.

I just thought you would like to know.

HENRY STEELE COMMONER
Middlebury, Conn.

EDITOR'S NOTE—*"Facts," wrote Macaulay, "are the mere dross of history." Dr. Commoner's letter is all too emblematic of the pedanticism of today's historians, who have discarded the great tradition of Tacitus, Gibbon, Parkman, Prescott, Motley, et al. in favor of a speciously "scientific" historiography. It so happens, however, that the "J.P.S." whose initials accompany the editorial in question was not the editor, but an unusually erudite taxi driver named Jonathan P. Snodgrass, now unfortunately deceased, who asked to be allowed to contribute an editorial. Since the Uneeda Review believes firmly in freedom of the press, the editor did not presume to alter the wording of his contribution.*

DEAR FRIEND,

You can well imagine both my surprise not to mention delight when reading your reviewer's most sympathetic not to say appreciative review of my *Years of Stunning Achievement Consistently Maintained: A History of the Uneeda Review.*

Reluctantly but stuck to my last like Ruskin's proverbial cobbler, I must point out one wee error: The landmark decision in *U.S. versus Bilbo's Dildo* was handed down in July 1976, not June. June and July look alot alike, and the words do too, I know, but, still, a fact is a fact.

Speaking of facts, I wonder how much longer I am going to have to put up with being accused of paranoid hallucinations every single time I mention however *sotto voce* and/or *en passant* that the world of art all the way from the Nobel Prize through the National Endowment down to the most modest soapcarver in darkest Arkansas is governed by a well-oiled and ancient secret conspiracy of Masons, Jews, Jesuits, and selected perverts from the P.L.O.? I mean, how much longer?

Jeepers: it was 52 years ago now that General Ludendorff blew his imperial Prussian whistle on the whole sordid affair, except he didn't have the P.L.O. to "reckon with," having nothing more (!) than Jesuits, Jewish bankers, and movie people, and Freemasons (esp. Scottish and York Rites) to give him a moment's pause. *The Coming War* was prophetic, and isn't it a shame Ludendorff—who was quoted by T. S. Eliot, no less, and published by Faber not to mention Faber—died before the coming war came?

This is no proverbial "bee in my belfry," hobby horse, or King Charles's head. Does nobody watch "Sesame Street"? Has nobody looked into the pedigree (?) of the likes of Blumenthal, Kissinger, Schlesinger, Habeeb, Ali McGraw, and both Shatner and Nimoy? Is the presence of Exodus in *Star Trek* invisible to all but the cultivated eye? Why does Woody Allen have all the money and all the Gentile girls and all the success and genius in the world? I mean, Portnoy finished what Mrs. Nussbaum started, or should I knuckle under like the rest of the passive sheep from sea to shining sea and say *Ms.* Nussbaum?

Let me ask you to ask yourself one very very simple question: Was Francis Scott Key a Jew? A Mason? A Jesuit? How (this is still the same one very very simple question) would the world-renowned author of the "Star-Spangled Banner" feel if he had to look at Yasir Arafat day in, day out? Does the man never shave? If not, why doesn't he look like he's grown a beard? What's all this betwixt-and-between stuff, facial hair wise? Whom does Jesse Helms think he's kidding?

Well. Thanx and a tip of the Hatlo Hat, as they used to say in the "funny papers" back when they were really *FUNNY* and not, i.e., in the hands of Feiffer and Trudeau who if they are not card-carrying Hebrew-Canadian-Jesuitico-Masons (or *Mapersons!*) they sure draw ''cartoons'' as though they sure could be.

TAFT TALMADGE
Asst. Prof. Emeritus of Tobacco Pest
Entomology, NCSU

QUEER CUR,

I worked I sweated blood on my blockbusting *The Eighth Marquess of Queensberry and How They Grew* and your reviewer well all I can say is is his/her name really Harper Bizarre?

First off I would of thought he/she would of known a Roman á clef when he/she laid eyes on one and why did he title his review ''New South Wails'' isn't that a place in Austria? I mean the historical M. of Q. lived from 1844–1900 which so did Nietzsche so why all the confusion as to whose who? The clef that my roman is á comes down to autobiography no French critic has been confused thereby. Its like saying no exercise is better than jogging or don't miss it if you can. Ironically I think I know in my head and heart too what he/she meant by that at the end.

While not claiming their no typoes or o-mees either in the hole tex of *TEMOQAHTG* it is as obvious as the nose on your/their face just besides the egg. You must think it cute to quote something less than verbatim and not put dots in to show the ''missing thumb'' on the ''pinochle hand'' so to as it were speak.

I can not believe that your reviewer really has never seen a book in which the events of 7 modern 24 hour pds. (the daze of the weak!!!) are subimposed under motifs from classical antiquity and their well-known myths such as Achilles or how

Orion (Urion) got his name according to Ovid. It was good for Paul and Silas and its good enough for me.

When Gertrude Stein died.

Yourn for more Specimen Days!
STINGO RARR

Carlysle Melanchthon

Uneeda Nimpossible Puzzle

THINK THICK!
DIAGRAMLESS
This quarter's rules: same as ever but multilingual puns possible, for example "crepuscular" (Fr.) leads to "twilit" which sounds like Fr. pron. of "toilet," backwards "teliot," hence "martyr in the catheter."

(Apologies for typo last quarter's clue #16 down, PARCEL POST should have been MARCEL PROUST ["Our hearts were young and——"].)

ACROSS

1. Sumo watched as Il Duce became staid.
6. Monks of a sort on bicycle built for 2 down.
11. Nobody's nose, the treble I've seen?
18. Lost chord? Not on your nelly!
28. Fanny Assingham offers semicolon to Uranus.
31. Latvian capital without first 49 stories.
40. Build thee more stately Mansons.
42. Free Rudolph Hess.
49. Tip a Canute and Tecumseh too.
55. Aftermath minus the math but no dice.
60. Soap is a thing with feathers.
75. Viva Darkbloom? Frozen water.
78. World book? En-cyclo-pedia beyond the hundredth hyphen.

1. Pope goes the weevil?
2. See 6 across.
8. Edgar Allan up short Ital. river.
11. No dice but some soap (soft?).
21. O. Possum "Impractical" Katz, e.g.
24. Not the Dover in Delaware nor in Arnold's opus.
30. By the tale, a tiger, added verbatim to Roman A-clef mandolin where Geo. Wallace bled one less air.
32. Aloha adobe abode?
35. I.e., vowels for no Russell.
39. *Lucus a non lucendo* corrupted to mean "It's called a missile because it doesn't miss."
56. Dimaggio, May, Mays, Lemay, and all their secret terces.

Uneeda Solution to Our Last Puzzle ("Jamesquare")

A	W	K	W	A	R	D	A	G	E
G	O	L	D	E	N	B	O	W	L
I	V	O	R	Y	T	O	W	E	R
N	E	N	U	P	H	A	R	E	Y
G	N	D	M	O	B	Y	D	I	K
A	S	Y	O	U	I	T	L	N	W
G	T	K	C	W	D	R	O	D	E
A	U	E	O	K	I	I	A	U	E
I	F	E	K	R	O	D	O	D	N
N	F	G	O	P	O	E	P	O	E

Note: three of HJ's titles fit the pattern "The" followed by two words in ten letters. We do not count *The Tragic Muse* because it is a miserable book.

Note: Special to "L.E., Honolulu": Your guesses are amusing but, fundamentally, all wet.

J. Parkhurst Schimmelpfennig as Peter Pan

Our Contributors

MABEL ARCH, beloved author of *Smiling Through, All Is Not Lost, Sweet Are the Uses of Adversity, Into Each Life, Understanding Disappointment, Living with Affliction, Making Bad Luck Work for You, Coping with Repeated Frustration, Demoralization from the Inside, I've Been There Myself, Good Tidings of Great Joy for the Alcoholic Spinster, Tell Me Not, Varicose Veins: An Intimate Portrait*, and the autobiographical *Only Daughter, Only Dad* committed suicide last December.

RODEO BARKIS practically invented Structuralism as a Field for Southpaws, Freaks, and Gay Blades.

MICHELANGELO BERMUDAS is Affirmative Action Professor of Metaphysics at the University of South Carolina at Florence in Florence, South Carolina. He says of his poetry: "I do it with others thing like as organ garding and my own weaving as well pots—just yesterday toss pots sixteen—now write English first—second transfer poem to native Xuro!klan—black third to idiomic English—am too short stop of softball and too base."

"EARL" is the nom de plume of Earl Earnhardt of Earl's Blems & Recaps, Earl Road, Earl, West Virginia ("just 2 mi. north of Resume Speed"). As a child, Mr. Earnhardt posed for Fisk advertisements, and to this day he ends all of his correspondence with "It's (yawn!) time to re-tire."

DILL EULENSPICKLE, who runs the Kukumber Press, is studying self-preservation at New Lyme Polytechnic Institute in Mount Olive, North Carolina.

NORTHCOTE FRICASSEE is a vegetable. He used to be an animal, and before that a Hegelian, and before than an amethyst, and before that the parliamentarian of an anarchist kraal, and before that a letter carrier in the suburbs of Pilotfish, Pennsylvania. He relates, "Lady up on Lakevista kept asking me if I was her male man? M-a-l-e. Ha-ha."

DESMOND GOOHOOLIGAN was a major figure in our cultural and literary life for a half century before his death a few years ago. Do we miss him? 'deed we do!

RODNEY GUGGENHEIM, now on his fourth Guggenheim, is living in Cuba and not poverty. He edited *Honesty* for one abortive issue and is now thriving as business manager of *Hypocrisy*.

Major BORESTONE HOOPLE has appeared in *AA Grapevine, Axilla's Armpit, Bazooka Backfire, Black Snowman, Copyright Infringement, Derivative Drivel, Extinct Species, Fat Domino, Felonious Monk, Frog Truck, Frying Tiger, Hurt Nurse, Index Prohibitorum, Joan Crawford's Shoulders, Local Focus Hocus-Pocus, Loose Lips, Magnolia Messerschmitt, Mobiter Dicta, Morning's Minion, Ovary, Peculiar Missouri, Platinum Maggot, Poughkeepsie Picayune, Saxifrage Marmalade, Tortured Orchard, Unique Phenomenon* (Akron), *Unique Phenomenon* (Dayton), *Unique Phenomenon* (Youngstown), *Visceral Linguistics,* and *You're Another;* but none of his writings have ever been published.

"Everybody Knows the Trouble I've Seen" is ALICE KIICKSTAND's latest effort. She is mostly known as the author of Twayne's *Pie Traynor* volume (TBPUS series).

BERNARDINO KORZENIOWSKI reports: "I am still a hit man."

LOCH LEMAN is full of it up to his neck. What is more, he is from Ponderosa, Calif.

RALPH LYING BULL sent the following on what looks like a piece of catamite hide: "You call me Indian one more time, I'll eat your liver. Indians are these creepy little schnooks who live on the Subcontinent with both a *Weltanschauung* and a life-style that would disgrace a savage and bloodthirsty Hottentot. And don't euphemize around with American Indian or pussyfoot with Amerind, either. It's like Wild Turkey Breath said to Andrew Jackson. I'll have you know that three-quarters of me is fullblooded Pequod, and I am gainfully employed as a Certified Public Native American with the state of New Mexico. Any anthropologistic weakblooded blue-eyed European immigrant who thinks he can call himself a native American just because he happens to be a native of America is patently, hopelessly, pitifully, and permanently *screwed up.*"

CARLYSLE MELANCHTHON is conceiver, founder, president-for-life, and laureate emeritus of the Circle of Bards, Scalds, Minstrels, Versifiers, and Other Incurable Lovers of the Muses of Anusmundi in the Autonomous People's Republic of Indiana. A recent recipient of the Anusmundi "Ten Thousand Sestinas" Certificate, he is doing twelve-to-fifteen in Terre Haute on a trumped-up charge of crime against nature.

LEONARD SCOTT MONGOOSE is renowned as the translator of so much loony French literature.

LEONIDAS O'DELL thinks he is Virginia Woolf, but instead he is only Elinor Glyn.

IOWA OLIVE is broadly beloved for her gentle but telling parodies of the semisurrealist symbolist lyrics of certain of her fellow midwesterners. She is credited with originating the old saying, "Carbondale, Illinois, is better than no noise at all." However, "If at first you don't suck seed, suck again" was said first by somebody else, she says, rather defensively.

JUDI PÊCHÉ tells us that she learned everything she knows at Oxford. "Now don't get confused. I mean Oxford, Ohio, where Miami is. Now don't get confused. I mean Miami of Ohio. It was at Oxford that I got the chance to work under ARNOLD BRUNT, who taught me alot about rhythm." When her job at Cornell (i.e., Cornell College in Mount Vernon, Iowa) became confusing, she moved—largely a matter of iambic monometer with a shifting caesura—to Indiana University of Pennsylvania, of which she says, "Now don't get confused. It's like Wyoming."

MORDRED ANATOL PENGUIN, having just completed a stretch as a staffer with the National Endowment for the Arts, has been awarded a National Endowment for the Arts fellowship to complete his unbiased appraisal of the overwhelming success of the National Endowment for the Arts. His first wife's second husband remains the blazing pyromaniac W. W. ("BURNT") NORTON, editor of the sensitive journal, *Arts Administration Morning Line.*

ST. JOHN PER SE of Baltimore and Key West worked for ten years on a book to be called *The Achievement of Hugh Kenner* but gave up after completing twenty-five words or less. So now he edits *I Am Very Very Bitter* on his mother's back porch "amongst forty-leven cats & ex-cats & near-cats."

GROGAN FURFUR PITT, lead soprano with the Pitt Family Singers, may be seen Thursday nights on their new television series, "The Pitts." Formerly rhythm guitar with the Scum of the Earth, he has written another new sonnet sequence, *Scum of the Earth,* published by Scum of the Earth Chapbooks, Ozone Park and Garden City, New York.

JOYCE CAROL O'SCHIMMELPFENNIG is not only poetry editor of *Uneeda Review,* but the daughter of the editor. She has appeared in this and every other literary journal for the past eleven years.

J. PARKHURST SCHIMMELPFENNIG, D.Ed., is author of *Poems New & Old, 1965-1983.* Don't miss it! (See ad, inside front cover)

In a wee tiny hand, OTIS SISTRUNK writes: "I am not, strictly speaking, *the* Otis Sistrunk. The real Otis Sistrunk, as you might say, has my freely given permission to continue the use of the name. I have submitted papers to change my name to Outis Sistrunk. That way Otis Sistrunk may stay out of confusion, hopefully. And yes—*thank* you very much *indeed* for inquiring—I still do grow championship parsnips in my goldfish bowl."

CRYSTAL SPANGLER is a mountain girl, best known for a quatrain she wrote at age 7 which got her expelled from Miss Tootie's Boarding and Finishing School for Young Ladies:

> I've never been to Lithia,
> I've never been to Grundy.
> But either place is busier
> Than Roanoke on a Sunday.

WILLIAM HARMON and LOUIS D. RUBIN, JR., under whose names some of this stuff has previously been published in various magazines, are imposters. They both live in Chapel Hill, North Carolina, a small village located along both sides of U.S. 15-501, where the principal sports are basketball, bird-watching, and money. Both teach at the University of North Carolina at Chapel Hill, a proprietary institution owned by Dean Smith.

By contrast, LEE SMITH, author of this issue's fiction, teaches at North Carolina State University, where it is real cool.

Classified Advertisements

Advertisements are accepted at the discretion of the publisher. No phone calls, please. Personal classified ads must be prepaid. $1.50 minimum three lines, 50¢ each additional ad. Advertisers requesting a box number will be charged an additional food stamp. Opinions expressed in these ads do not necessarily represent the opinion of the management; on the other hand, who knows . . . ?

Instruction

THE MAN THAT HATH no music in his soul is fit for treason, stratagems, and spoils. Be the life of the party! Learn how to play blues guitar. Write W.S., c/o Hartford Accident & Indemnity Co., Hartford, Conn.

WILL EXCHANGE navigation lessons for the tutoring in English. J.C., Stanford-le-Hope, Sussex, Eng.

HOW DOES YOUR GARDEN grow? Don't contaminate your vegetables with lethal chemicals. Learn how to use organic fertilizer for superior gardening. Write Stetson, Mylae, c/o Faber & Faber, London, Eng.

MAKE LOVE WITH FLOWERS! New ideas for exotic arrangements, unusual ways to display forget-me-nots, campion buds, bluebells, hyacinths, etc. For details write Chatterly, Wragby, Tevershall, Eng.

HAVING TROUBLE REMEMBERING TO WIND grandfather clocks? Send 50¢ plus self-addressed stamped envelope for details of infallible method, guaranteed to make you remember when clock-winding time comes. Write L. Sterne, Cotswould, Yorkshire, Eng.

POET wishes swimming lessons. Will swap for inscribed copy first book. Write Crane, Box 23K.

Wanted To Buy or Lease

URGENT! Must have ticket for performance of "Our American Cousin," Ford's Theater, April 14. Will pay top price. Write Booth, c/o Surratt's Boarding House, H St., Washington, D.C.

WOULD WHOEVER cut and stacked approximately one cord maple firewood and left same in swamp three miles north of town be interested in selling same? Contact R.F., RFD 2, Derry, N.H.

WANT TO BUY sailboat in good condition. Prefer gaff-topsail rig. Write Shelley, Spezzia, Italia.

WISH TO PURCHASE several iron window sashes. Cash, or will swap for watch, still running but needs hands, crystal. See Q.C., Hollis Hall, Harvard Yard, Cambridge, Mass.

NEED DOZEN LIFEBOATS in good condition. Must be delivered in time for arrival new passenger liner due April 18. For specifications call or write White Star Lines, NYC.

WISH TO RENT set of velvet drapery, bust of Pallas Athene, talking crow, for two-week period. Will insure. Write E.A.P., c/o *Broadway Journal,* NYC.

Help Wanted

HAVE VACANCY for several experienced seamen for three-year voyage Pacific, Indian Oceans, etc. Exceptional captain, comfortable quarters, all benefits. Apply in person, Capts. Bildad or Peleg, *Pequod,* Nantucket, Mass.

VACANCY for capable woman to serve as governess, tutor for two children at country estate. References required. *Important: Must Not Be Novel Reader.* Apply 57, Harley St., London, Eng.

For Sale

USED BEDSTEAD in good shape. Write c/o Hathaway, Stratford-on-Avon, Eng.

CHRISTMAS is a-coming! For good buy in imported fruit, call Eugenides, Hotel Metropole, London, Eng.

Lost and Found

LOST, in vicinity of Hofburg, envelope containing two symphonic movements, marked III, IV. Valuable to owner only. Write F. Schubert, Neue Wieden, Vienna.

Personals

WILL THE PARTY who witnessed fatal accident involving yellow Rolls-Royce near Wilson's Garage, Rt. 25, Long Island, Sunday please call the undersigned at once? Important. N.V. Carraway, 1232 (East Egg exch.).

WOULD MEDICAL STUDENT like to share Martello Tower? No panthers or Englishmen allowed. Nonpoet preferred, but will consider ballad-writer. Bring your own snotrag. S.D., Box 72, Dublin, Ire.

ANNETTE V.: called home, will return soon as possible. Advise if coast is clear. Your WILLIE.

NEED SOMEONE who really cares? Attractive brunette has what it takes. Interested Chinoiserie, Vermeer, can play piano. Either sex. Your place anytime, my place appointment only. Call 21-13-34, ask for Odette de C.

LOVERS OF FINER THINGS in life. Companionable girl, 30s, English nobility, seeks lasting relationship with man of feeling. Must have wealth. May be war veteran, but if wounded, detailed medical report required. Write or wire B.A., c/o Hotel Montana, Madrid, Spain.

H.P. Darling, feel helpless. Tell me if can do anything. Yours for eternity, ARTHUR. P.S. If need money, advise.

Lady Vaseline Morale-Schimmelpfennig as Alice

NEW FROM SANITARY BOOKS

Hugs Kenner: POUND'S SOUNDS
"Nobody can ken like Kenner can."
—Wm. F. Bulky

Ma Jong: PUDENDUM UNDER GLASS: A
NONFICTION NAVEL
"What a gal! She's a real comer!"
—Pa Jong

William Hardon: WAN JONG YAWN: *Poems*
"Dodecaphonic Algorithms for Brass and
Percussion. Hardon is the James Dickey
of the South."
—George Coarse

Paul De Mann: DE GUSTIBUS AIN'T WHAT
DEY USED T'BE: DE FROG IN DE
WOODPILE
"Even better than *De Derrida à Diderot*—a
tour de force that through the green
few drives the flour."
—Loose Ruby, Jr.

Elmo Fudd: RUDD, MUDD, AND JUDD:
TV NEWS IN THE AGE OF GAGA
"The kind of thing you'll like if you really
like this kind of thing."
—Kirkus

Michael Hen-Shaw: THE MARE OF
     CASTERBRIDGE: HARDY'S HIDDEN
     HORSES
     ''Up to the rare standard set by his earlier
     Somebody Bet on the Bay Rum!''
           —Helen Vendling-Machine

Hairoil Blum: MAB: ON MS.-READING
     ''He's done it again.''
           —Rabbit Pen (Warren)

Herpes Trismegistus, M.D.: FOODLESS
     COOKING—THE ULTIMATE DIET
     ''Lots of lo-cal color. Will do for pudgepots
     what Jean Harris did for Tarnower.''
           —*Mademoiselle*

At Good Bookstores Everywhere!

Discover how grinning faces, beheading matrons, strange beasts with huge claws and waving tentacles, mysterious unguents, deformed children with monstrous necks and limbs, fractured panes of glass, snakes, eels, babies that become grunting beasts, sinister mushrooms, strangely labeled jars, explosive sneezes and shrieks, furious tantrums, figure in the nightmarish dreams of a little girl.

Every parent of a teen-age or pre-teen-age daughter should read this astounding narrative! Learn what YOUR child may be thinking! You'll be amazed . . . and appalled!

Hurry down to your bookstore and buy Lewis Carroll's sensational *Alice in Wonderland.* Wayward House, $9.95.